Wisdom of One

The Ultimate Existentialist Quote Book

Compiled and Edited by
Thomas E. Kelly

Hara Publishing
Seattle, WA

ACKNOWLEDGMENTS

For their contributions, both direct and indirect, my very special thanks to:

Francis Bomer, Beth Buck, Cheryl Carr, Jennie Carstensen, Felix Cross, Jon Curry, Trevor Fitz-Gibbon, Tim Freccia, Nik Hanson, Leo Heckmann, Cassie Hillman, Denise Johnson, Lorraine Johnson, JoAnne Kelly, Lee Kelly, Jen Linden, Kai Neumann, Len Sampson, Jen Willson

... and to my friends in Switzerland — including Frédo — who unknowingly revealed to me my own philosophy ...

INTRODUCTION

Since it was coined earlier this century, the term *existentialism* has been largely misused and misunderstood. Deemed a brooding and nihilistic phase of postwar literature, it has suffered from the narrow definition lent it in classrooms and coffeehouses alike. What most people don't realize is that most existentialists maintained a highly *optimistic* approach to life in the present, and that their motto, if they had one, would probably have been "Seize the day!" This runs contrary to most everything one hears on the subject, but then it has also been scarcely acknowledged that the basic principles of existentialism are of a timeless nature, and can be traced back at least as far as ancient Greece and Rome. This way of thinking is hardly a modern one; but rather a philosophy which has developed and repeated itself intermittently since the birth of man.

Thus, as you absorb this collection, I'm sure you'll come across scores of quotes by people who have never been viewed as existentialists per se. From Shakespeare to Beethoven to Picasso, my criteria in selecting them was simply that they be consistent with the overall themes of Solitude, Self-Determination, Aesthetic Beauty, and the limitless possibilities afforded us by life in the Present. Not that I have excluded sections on the darker side of existence, but have attempted, rather, to replace the myths and misconceptions surrounding existentialism with a definition better suited to our times.

Of those labels typically affixed to the word *existentialist,* "nihilist," "fatalist," and "pessimist" are certainly among the most frequently employed. It seems ironic, therefore, that nearly all those writers associated with the movement constantly sought the refuge of beauty, joy, and deep spiritual gratification during their lifetimes. Admittedly, a preoccupation with the darker side of existence is manifest in the works of Sartre, Camus, Dostoevsky and Kafka, to name a few. Converse to appearances, however, each was in his own way resigned wholly to life—one has only to read their personal journals to confirm this.

Further, although most of these authors believed in the total cessation of life after death, I would posit on their behalf that belief in nothing *afterwards* does not constitute nihilism. The absence of any definitive future, instead, consigns one fully to the present, to this day in which we are living, to life itself. In acknowledging the "Now" or "Never" of existence, we must, out of self-respect, choose "Now." In acknowledging an end to everything, we are each confined to our own Something. In acknowledging the "No" of eternity, we are saying "Yes" to life! Thus, although they digress from the more "traditional" concepts of anguish, death, and despair, the sections on Love, Happiness, and Beauty in this anthology are very much justified. Hence the inclusion of authors such as Hemingway and Rand, who conveyed the individual's need of pleasure amidst all the suffering sustained in this life, and demonstrated the vividness of human existence against a background of darker elements.

Despite attempts to classify existentialists and group them together, the only thing that writers like Nietzsche, Rilke, Kierkegaard and de Beauvoir had in common was their *departure* from popular philosophies and religions, and their hailing of the Individual over Society. Beyond this, they all agreed on very little, and tended each to follow their own path. Indeed, the words of Erasmus, "Every definition is dangerous," ring especially true in the case of existentialism. "By definition," existentialism maintains paradoxically that every man is free to determine his own personalized view of existence, to create his own meaning of life.

This, of course, is by no means an idea born of the past 150 years. Viewed simply as an approach adopted by rebels, it becomes nearly impossible to trace the roots of existentialism back to any single time or group of individuals. Looking back, scores of historic figures rose from the ashes of isolation and solitude to create their own phoenix of existence. From Epicurus to Emerson and Sophocles to Sartre; irrespective of the epoch, each considered a man as the source of his own actions, and each ascribed to only one doctrine: his own.

Thus, never as a philosophy was existentialism intended to show men *why* or *how* to live, beyond revealing to them that it lay in their own power to *choose*. "Be a man," exclaimed Nietzsche, "and do not follow me—but yourself!" To create one's own destiny—to fill in the blank—the challenge of existence has always been the same. And to teach and inspire *by example* has always been the key to unleashing individual strengths and powers. To my mind, nothing is better suited to this task than the quote.

— Thomas E. Kelly
Seattle, 1995

ABILITY and ACHIEVEMENT

All serious daring starts from within.

— EUDORA WELTY

The world is all gates, all opportunities, strings of tension waiting to be struck.

— EMERSON

It had long since come to my attention that people of accomplishment rarely sat back and let things happen to them. They went out and happened to things.

— ELINOR SMITH

Do what you can, with what you have, where you are.

— THEODORE ROOSEVELT

The activity itself is less important than the act of drawing upon your own resources.

— BARBARA GORDON

The reward of a thing well done is to have done it.

— EMERSON

To achieve great things, we must live as though we were never going to die.

— VAUVENARGUES

ACTION

A man is the origin of his action.

— ARISTOTLE

Man's destiny, then, is primarily action.

— JOSE ORTEGA Y GASSET

There is no reality except in action. — SARTRE

In *esse* I am nothing. In *posse* I am everything.
— JOHN ADAMS

Action takes on the presence of a work of art.
— JEAN COCTEAU

All the beautiful sentiments in the world weigh less than a single lovely action. — J.R. LOWELL

Action is eloquence. — SHAKESPEARE

Two things were impossible to him: to stand still or to move aimlessly. — AYN RAND

It is in your act that you exist, not in your body. Your act is yourself, and there is no other you.
— SAINT-EXUPERY

We become just by performing just actions, temperate by performing temperate actions, brave by performing brave actions. — ARISTOTLE

Action is the only reality; not only reality but morality as well. — ABBIE HOFFMAN

He who desires, but acts not, breeds pestilence.
— WILLIAM BLAKE

Give me the storm and tempest of thought and action, rather than the dead calm of ignorance and faith.
— ROBERT INGERSOLL

Our nature lies in movement; absolute rest is death.
— BLAISE PASCAL

To know and to act are one and the same.
— SAMURAI MAXIM

It is the mark of a good action that it appears inevitable in the retrospect.   — ROBERT LOUIS STEVENSON

Act is virgin. Even repeated.   — RENE CHAR

Action is the function of one. — CHARLES de GAULLE

AESTHETICS

Only as an aesthetic phenomenon may existence and the world appear justified.   — NIETZSCHE

For my part, in life (or in death) there are no reasons but esthetic reasons.   — JUAN RAMON JIMENEZ

Ethics and aesthetics are one and the same.
— LUDWIG WITTGENSTEIN

AGE and AGING

A man who is young in years may be old in hours, if he has lost no time.   — FRANCIS BACON

We grow neither better nor worse as we get old, but more like ourselves.   — MAY LAMBERTON BECKER

The worst thing, I fear, about being no longer young, is that one is no longer young.   — HAROLD NICHOLSON

Old or young, we are all on our last cruise.
                                          — ROBERT LOUIS STEVENSON

ANSWERS

Questions show the mind's range, and answers its subtlety.   — JOSEPH JOUBERT

If there are questions then, of course, there are answers, but the final answer makes the questions seem absurd.
                                          — JOHN CAGE

In the last analysis, it is our conception of death which decides our answers to all the questions that life puts to us.   — DAG HAMMARSKJOLD

There ain't no answer. There ain't going to be any answer. There never has been an answer. That's the answer.   — GERTRUDE STEIN

The shortest answer is doing.   — GEORGE HERBERT

The only interesting answers are those which destroy the questions. No answer—no matter how persuasive—will ever have enough strength to resist indefinitely the question that sooner or later will come to summon it.
                                          — EDMOND JABES

4

An answer is always a form of death. — JOHN FOWLES

APPEARANCES

Being means appearing.   — HEIDEGGER

Appearances are beautiful in their momentary truth.
                                          — OCTAVIO PAZ

The appearance is not supported by any existent different from itself; it has its own being.   — SARTRE

There is no frontier between being and appearing.
                                          — CAMUS

It is the bright, the bold, the transparent who are clever-
est among those who are silent: their ground is down so
deep that even the brightest water does not betray it.
                                          — NIETZSCHE

It is only shallow people who do not judge by appearances; the true mystery of the world is the visible, not
the invisible.   — OSCAR WILDE

Things are entirely what they appear to be and *behind
them*...there is nothing.   — SARTRE

Do not, I beg you, look for anything behind phenomena.
They are themselves their own lesson.   — GOETHE

That which is not apparent does not exist.
                                          — LEGAL MAXIM

ARGUMENTS and ARGUING

I have won every argument I ever had with myself.
— WILLIAM FEATHER

It was completely fruitless to quarrel with the world, whereas the quarrel with oneself was occasionally fruitful and always, she had to admit, interesting.
— MAY SARTON

ART and ARTISTS

Art is essentially the affirmation, the blessing, and the deification of existence.
— NIETZSCHE

Art is a higher type of knowledge than experience.
— ARISTOTLE

Art never expresses anything but itself.
— OSCAR WILDE

I wanted to become a work of art myself, and not an artist.
— BERNARD BERENSON

Individuality of expression is the beginning and ending of all art.
— GOETHE

An artist is a man of action, whether he creates a personality, invents an expedient, or finds the issue of a complicated situation.
— JOSEPH CONRAD

I will maintain that the artist needs this: a special world of which he alone has the key.
— ANDRE GIDE

A work of art has no importance whatever to society. It is only important to the individual. — NABOKOV

All art is a revolt against man's fate.
— ANDRE MALRAUX

We have art in order not to die of the truth.
— NIETZSCHE

If the world were clear, art would not exist. — CAMUS

All art is the same—an attempt to fill an empty space.
— SAMUEL BECKETT

Art is nothing. A little bit of nothing. — LARRY RIVERS

No artist desires to prove anything. — OSCAR WILDE

The morality of art is in its very beauty.
— GUSTAVE FLAUBERT

Art is the only thing that can go on mattering once it has stopped hurting. — ELIZABETH BOWEN

Music exists...only in motion. The good listener will hear it as the present prolonged. — NED ROREM

I do evolve, *I am*. In art there is neither past nor future. Art that is not in the present will never be. — PICASSO

Music is immediate. It goes on to become.
— W. H. AUDEN

The camera makes everyone a tourist in other people's reality, and eventually in one's own. — SUSAN SONTAG

All art deals with the absurd and aims at the simple.
— IRIS MURDOCH

An artist is a dreamer consenting to dream of the actual world. — SANTAYANA

What we play is life. — LOUIS ARMSTRONG

Every portrait that is painted with feeling is a portrait of the artist, not the sitter. — OSCAR WILDE

Nothing can come out of the artist that is not in the man.
— H. L. MENCKEN

The essential feature of art is its power of perfecting existence. — NIETZSCHE

The ultimate function of art is to make men do what they want to do, as it is to make them recognize what they know. — MAURICE BLONDEL

Art is a mirror which is "fast" like a watch—sometimes.
— KAFKA

All art is at once surface and symbol. Those who go beneath the surface do so at their own peril.
— OSCAR WILDE

Nothing is likely about masterpieces, least of all whether there will be any. — IGOR STRAVINSKY

O young artist, you search for a subject...Your subject is
yourself. — EUGENE DELACROIX

Art does not reproduce the visible; rather, it makes
visible. — PAUL KLEE

No artist is ahead of his time. He is his time.
— MARTHA GRAHAM

All works of art should begin...at the end.
— EDGAR ALLEN POE

Art teaches nothing, except the significance of life.
— HENRY MILLER

ATHEISM and ATHEISTS

An atheist is a man who has no invisible means of support. — JOHN BUCHAN

I am an atheist still, thank God. — LUIS BUNUEL

Existentialism isn't so atheistic that it wears itself out
showing that God does not exist. Rather, it declares that
even if God did exist, that would change nothing.
— SARTRE

If there is a God, atheism must strike Him as less of an
insult than religion.
— EDMOND et JULES de GONCOURT

The complete atheist stands on the penultimate step to
the most perfect faith. — DOSTOEVSKY

I have no higher idea than my disbelief in God.
— DOSTOEVSKY

She believed in nothing; only her skepticism kept her from being an atheist.　— SARTRE

Atheism and a kind of *second innocence* belong together.
— NIETZSCHE

BEAUTY

Anything in any way beautiful derives its beauty from itself, and asks nothing beyond itself.
— MARCUS AURELIUS

They are the elect to whom beautiful things mean only Beauty.　— OSCAR WILDE

To keep beauty in its place is to make all things beautiful.
— SANTAYANA

Things are not done beautifully. The beauty is an integral part of their being done.　— ROBERT HENRI

In the depths of our darkness there is no one place for Beauty. The whole place is for Beauty.　— RENE CHAR

Though we travel the world over to find the beautiful, we must carry it with us or we find it not. — EMERSON

With beauty you have to live (and die) alone.
— JUAN RAMON JIMENEZ

Beauty is unbearable, drives us to despair, offering us for a minute the glimpse of an eternity that we should like to stretch over the whole of time.   — CAMUS

Beauty is feared / more than death.
                    — WILLIAM CARLOS WILLIAMS

If I had to choose between beauty and truth, I should not hesitate; it is beauty that I should keep, feeling sure that it bears within it a truth loftier and more profound than truth itself.   — ANATOLE FRANCE

Beauty is an ecstasy; it is as simple as hunger. There is really nothing to be said about it.
                    — W. SOMERSET MAUGHAM

"Beauty is truth, truth beauty,"—that is all / Ye know on earth, and all ye need to know.   — JOHN KEATS

Beauty is its own excuse for being.   — EMERSON

Nothing beautiful can be separated from life, and it is life itself that dies.   — PAUL VALERY

It is because everything must come to an end that everything is so beautiful.   — CHARLES RAMUZ

Verily, it is not in satiety that his desire shall grow silent and be submerged, but in beauty.   — NIETZSCHE

And Beauty is a form of Genius—is higher, indeed, than Genius, as it needs no explanation.   — OSCAR WILDE

Beauty will save the world.   — DOSTOEVSKY

We ascribe beauty to that which is simple; which has no superfluous parts; which exactly answers its ends.
     — EMERSON

Everywhere is beauty and nowhere permanence... nowhere an intention, nor a responsibility, nor a plan.
     — SANTAYANA

When you have only two pennies left in the world, buy a loaf of bread with one, and a lily with the other.
     — CHINESE PROVERB

But beauty, real beauty, ends where the intellect begins.
     — OSCAR WILDE

Beauty, O thou, may thy name always be blest, / thy will be done, thy kingdom come. Earth shall / worship thee and no other god!   — JACQUES PERK

A thing of beauty is a joy for ever: / Its loveliness increases; it will never / pass into nothingness.
     — JOHN KEATS

In beauty it is finished. / In beauty it is finished.
     — NAVAJO REFRAIN

BEGINNING and END

Men perish because they cannot join the beginning with the end.   — ALCAMAEON

The acts of life have neither beginning nor end.
                                    — TRISTAN TZARA

There is no end. There is no beginning. There is only
the infinite passion of life.   — FEDERICO FELLINI

We can depend much more upon reaching an end than
on coming from a beginning.
                                    — JUAN RAMON JIMENEZ

We can ask primal questions, but we can never stand
near the beginning.   — KARL JASPERS

Nothing, of course, begins at the time you think it did.
                                    — LILLIAN HELLMAN

I am an end or a beginning.   — KAFKA

The realization that life is absurd cannot be seen as an
end, but only as a beginning.   — CAMUS

Not every end is the goal.   — NIETZSCHE

BOOKS and READING

A novel is never anything but a philosophy put into
images.   — CAMUS

Every page is a paper mirror. You bend over it and look
at yourself.   — EDMOND JABES

For the creation of a masterwork of literature two powers must concur; the power of the man and the power of the moment.   — MATTHEW ARNOLD

All good books are alike in that they are truer than if they really happened and after you are finished reading one you will feel that it all happened to you, and afterwards it all belongs to you.   — HEMINGWAY

If this book had not fallen into my hands at the precise moment it did, perhaps I would have gone mad.
           — HENRY MILLER

There is nothing so important as the book *can* be.
           — MAXWELL PERKINS

I can find my biography in every fable that I read.
           — EMERSON

I never travel without my diary. One should always have something sensational to read on the train.
           — OSCAR WILDE

Every man with a belly full of the classics is an enemy of the human race.   — HENRY MILLER

The more I read, the more I meditate; and the more I acquire, the more I am enabled to affirm that I know nothing.   — VOLTAIRE

Fiction reveals truth that reality obscures.
           — JESSAMYN WEST

Literature is born when something in life goes slightly adrift. — SIMONE de BEAUVOIR

For the most part, our novel-reading is a passion for results. — EMERSON

The final test for a novel will be our affection for it, as it is the test of our friends, and of anything which we cannot define. — E. M. FORSTER

This book became my friend because it taught me that I had no need of friends. — HENRY MILLER

It had become the book of which I never spoke: perfection seals our lips. — CAMUS

BREVITY

To be brief is almost a condition of being inspired. — SANTAYANA

To be brief is the supreme morality of art. — JUAN RAMON JIMENEZ

CALM

Still, there is a calm, pure harmony, and music inside of me. — VINCENT van GOGH

Back of tranquility there lies always conquered unhappiness. — DAVID GRAYSON

When we are unable to find tranquility within ourselves, it is useless to seek it elsewhere.
— FRANCOIS de la ROCHEFOUCAULD

Nothing can bring you peace but yourself. — EMERSON

There is no joy but calm. — ALFRED, LORD TENNYSON

Calmer and calmer.
— J.F.C. von SCHILLER (last words)

CERTAINTY and UNCERTAINTY

Certainty generally is illusion, and repose is not the destiny of man.
— OLIVER WENDELL HOLMES

The quest for certainty blocks the search for meaning. Uncertainty is the very condition to impel man to unfold his powers.
— ERICH FROMM

I am frightened by the certainties that reign around me.
— BERNARD FONTENELLE

Without a measureless and perpetual uncertainty, the drama of human life would be destroyed.
— WINSTON CHURCHILL

Maturity is the capacity to endure uncertainty.
— JOHN FINLEY

That which needs to be proved cannot be worth much.
— NIETZSCHE

There are no facts, only interpretations. — NIETZSCHE

Certitude drives mad. — NIETZSCHE

You are all you will ever have for certain.
— JUNE HAVOC

Unrest and uncertainty are our lot. — GOETHE

CHANGE

A permanent state of transition is man's most noble condition. — JUAN RAMON JIMENEZ

The moment of change is the only poem.
— ADRIENNE RICH

The man who does not look at his change is no true poet.
— G. K. CHESTERTON

All changes, even the most longed for, have their melancholy; for what we leave behind us is a part of ourselves; we must die to one life before we can enter another. — ANATOLE FRANCE

People change and forget to tell each other.
— LILLIAN HELLMAN

When you get there, there isn't any there there.
— GERTRUDE STEIN

To live is change, and to be perfect is to have changed often. — JOHN HENRY NEWMAN

Loss is nothing else but change, and change is Nature's delight. — MARCUS AURELIUS

Nothing endures but change. (All is flux, nothing stays still.) — HERACLITUS

Transition is a complete present which unites the past and the future in a momentary progressive ecstasy, a progressive eternity, a true eternity of eternities, the eternal moments. — JUAN RAMON JIMENEZ

CHAOS and CONFUSION

Confusion is a word we have invented to explain an order which is not understood. — HENRY MILLER

The confusion is not my invention...it is all around us and our only chance is to let it in. — SAMUEL BECKETT

I tell you: one must still have chaos in one, to give birth to a dancing star. — NIETZSCHE

We live in a rainbow of chaos. — PAUL CEZANNE

The torch of doubt and chaos, this is what the sage steers by. — CHUANG TZU

From the beginning it was never anything but chaos: it was a fluid which enveloped me, which I breathed in through the gills. — HENRY MILLER

... and he was almighty because he had wrenched from chaos the secret of its nothingness. — SARTRE

Chaos often breeds life, where order breeds habit. — HENRY ADAMS

Chaos is the score upon which reality is written. — HENRY MILLER

Man fixes some wonderful erection of his own between himself and the wild chaos, and gradually goes bleached and stifled under his parasol. Then comes a poet, enemy of convention, and makes a slit in the umbrella; and lo! the glimpse of chaos is a vision, a window to the sun. — D. H. LAWRENCE

CHARACTER

Character is destiny. — SPANISH PROVERB

If one has character one also has one's typical experience which recurs again and again. — NIETZSCHE

This is the mark of a perfect character—to pass through each day as though it were the last, without agitation, without torpor, and without pretense. — MARCUS AURELIUS

Talent develops in quiet places, character in the full current of human life. — GOETHE

CHILDREN

One must ask children and birds how strawberries and
cherries taste. — GOETHE

Childhood is the kingdom where nobody dies.
— EDNA ST. VINCENT MILLAY

"Did you have a happy childhood?" is a false question.
As a child I did not know what happiness was, and
whether I was happy or not. I was too busy *being.*
— ALISTAIR REID

Children are the true connoisseurs. What's precious to
them has no price—only value. — BEL KAUFMAN

CHOICE

I do not create myself, I choose myself.
— KIERKEGAARD

You are free, therefore choose...that is to say, invent.
— SARTRE

What man wants is simply *independent* choice, whatever
that independence may cost and wherever it may lead.
— DOSTOEVSKY

The flower you single out is a rejection of all other flowers; nevertheless, only on these terms is it beautiful.
— SAINT-EXUPERY

One cannot weep for the entire world. It is beyond human strength. One must choose. — JEAN ANOUILH

There are countless roads on all sides of the grave.
— CICERO

When making your choice in life, do not forget to live.
— SAMUEL JOHNSON

CIRCUMSTANCE

I am myself plus my circumstance and if I do not save it, I cannot save myself. — JOSE ORTEGA Y GASSETT

I am the circumstance. — OCTAVIO PAZ

Circumstances! I make circumstances! — NAPOLEON I

Circumstances are the creatures of men.
— BENJAMIN DISRAELI

COLORS

The purest and most thoughtful minds are those which love colour the most. — JOHN RUSKIN

Death and colors are things we cannot discuss.
— CAMUS

COMMUNICATION

There is no such thing as conversation. It is an illusion. There are intersecting monologues, that is all.
— REBECCA WEST

Communication, if it is required, is a way of calling attention to one's own psychology.
— JOHN CAGE

True communication excludes all other possibilities.
— KARL JASPERS

CONSCIENCE

They talk of a man betraying his country, his friends, his sweet-heart. There must be a moral bond first. All a man can betray is his conscience.
— JOSEPH CONRAD

The one thing that doesn't abide by majority rule is a person's conscience.
— HARPER LEE

A state of conscience is higher than a state of innocence.
— THOMAS MANN

I cannot and will not cut my conscience to suit this year's fashions.
— LILLIAN HELLMAN

The man who can really stand alone in the world, only taking counsel from his conscience—that man is a hero.
— KIERKEGAARD

CONSCIOUSNESS

For everything begins with consciousness and nothing is worth anything except through it. — CAMUS

Consciousness is a being, the nature of which is to be conscious of the nothingness of its being. — SARTRE

To be too conscious is an illness—a real thorough-going illness. — DOSTOEVSKY

Lucidity is the wound nearest the sun. — RENE CHAR

The aim of life is to live, and to live means to be aware, joyously, drunkenly, serenely, divinely aware.
— HENRY MILLER

Renounce your consciousness and you become a brute.
— AYN RAND

To be conscious that we are perceiving or thinking is to be conscious of our own existence. — ARISTOTLE

Consciousness...can only take on the form of the cavity it fills. — R. M. ALBERES

Consciousness reigns but does not govern.
— PAUL VALERY

CONSISTENCY and INCONSISTENCY

No thinker has ever...said that a change of mind was inconsistency. — CICERO

Do I contradict myself? / Very well then, I contradict myself. / I am large; I contain multitudes.

— WALT WHITMAN

I have my faults, but changing my tune is not one of them.

— SAMUEL BECKETT

To be honest, one must be inconsistent. — H. G. WELLS

Don't be consistent, but be simply true.

— OLIVER WENDALL HOLMES

Consistency is the last refuge of the unimaginative.

— OSCAR WILDE

The man who sees only one source knows only one storm. The chances in himself are thwarted.

— RENE CHAR

With consistency a great soul has simply nothing to do.

— EMERSON

CREATION and CREATIVITY

He who has to be creator always has to destroy.

— NIETZSCHE

Creative minds have always been known to survive any kind of bad training.   — ANNA FREUD

To create is likewise to shape to one's fate.   — CAMUS

If you have creative work, you don't have age or time.
— LOUISE NEVELSON

Creating is living doubly.   — CAMUS

True happiness is man's own creation—making one's
emotions independent of one's own fate.
— WILHELM von HUMBOLDT

The creator is not concerned with disease—but with life.
— AYN RAND

The DARKNESS of BEING

We penetrated deeper and deeper into the heart of darkness. It was very quiet there.   — JOSEPH CONRAD

Let me hear nothing of the moon, for in my night there
is no moon, and if it happens that I speak of the stars it is
by mistake.   — SAMUEL BECKETT

There is no sun without shadow, and it is essential to
know the night.   — CAMUS

In the real dark night of the soul it is always three o'clock
in the morning.   — F. SCOTT FITZGERALD

Actually, light dazzles me. I only keep enough of it in me
to look at the night, the whole of nights, all nights.
— PAUL ELUARD

To confront a person with his shadow is to show him his
own light.   — CARL JUNG

Everyone is a moon and has a dark side which he never shows to anybody. — MARK TWAIN

And when you gaze long into the abyss the abyss also gazes into you. — NIETZSCHE

It's the night that looks at you, but it's a dazzling night, in fullest splendor; the night behind the day.— SARTRE

I owe allegiance to the race of those / who from the dark aspire to clarity. — GOETHE

In a dark time, the eye begins to see. — ROETHKE

DEATH and DYING

When I think of death it's with a view to living—not to dying. — ANDRE MALRAUX

Death, the most dreaded of evils, is therefore of no concern to us; for while we exist death is not present, and when death is present we no longer exist.— EPICURUS

The whole motley confusion of acts, omissions, regrets and hopes which is the life of each one of us finds in death, not meaning or explanation, but an end. — OCTAVIO PAZ

One should part from life as Odysseus parted from Nausicaa—blessing it rather than in love with it. — NIETZSCHE

And if the earthly no longer knows your name, /
whisper to the silent earth: I'm flowing. / To the flashing
water say: I am.   — RANIER MARIA RILKE

There is nothing after death, and death itself is nothing.
                                    — SENECA

Man dies when he wants, as he wants, of what he
chooses.   — JEAN ANOUILH

Our final experience, like our first, is conjectural. We
move between two darknesses.   — E. M. FORSTER

My theory tells us that ours is the power to invent the
very world we are quitting...it is as if the bird could die
in flight.   — JOHN HAWKES

Man imagines that it is death he fears; but what he fears
is the unforeseen, the explosion. What man fears is
himself.   — SAINT-EXUPERY

To die is poignantly bitter, but the idea of having to die
without having lived is unbearable. — ERICH FROMM

Do not fear death so much, but rather the inadequate
life.   — BERTOLT BRECHT

The dark background which death supplies brings out
the tender colors of life in all their purity.
                                    — SANTAYANA

The brave man dies perhaps two thousand deaths if he's
intelligent.   — HEMINGWAY

Let us beware of saying that death is the opposite of life.

— NIETZSCHE

Foolish, therefore, is the man who says that he fears death, not because it will pain when it comes, but because it pains in the prospect. — EPICURUS

He who most resembles the dead is the most reluctant to die. — JEAN de la FONTAINE

Dying / is an art, like everything else. — SYLVIA PLATH

The act of dying is also one of the acts of life.

— MARCUS AURELIUS

The thought of death is a nimble dancer. Everybody is too serious for me. — KIERKEGAARD

That your dying be no blasphemy against man and earth, my friends, that I ask of the honey of your soul.

— NIETZSCHE

Be absolute for death. — SHAKESPEARE

Death becomes the meaning of life as the resolved chord is the meaning of the melody. — SARTRE

Dying is not everything: you have to die in time.

— SARTRE

We are wrong in looking forward to death: in great measure it is past already. — SENECA

Death is not anything...death is not...It's the absence of presence, nothing more...the endless time of never coming back...a gap you can't see, and when the wind blows through it, it makes no sound. — TOM STOPPARD

Death speaks to us with a deep voice but has nothing to say. — PAUL VALERY

Dead is dead yes dead is really dead yes to be dead is to be really dead yes to be dead is to really be dead.
— GERTRUDE STEIN

Every death even the cruellest death / drowns in the total indifference of Nature. — PETER WEISS

I believe that when I die I shall rot, and nothing of my ego will survive...But I should scorn to shiver with terror at the thought of annihilation. Happiness is nonetheless true happiness because it must come to an end, nor do thought and love lose their value because they are not everlasting. — BERTRAND RUSSELL

All interest in disease and death is only another expression of interest in life. — THOMAS MANN

It seems to me that I am staking myself, all that I am, on a single moment—my last. — ANDRE MALRAUX

And cessation is what we seek, if only because it alone is utterly unbelievable. — JOHN HAWKES

Death is just infinity closing in. — JORGE LUIS BORGES

Death destroys a man, the idea of Death saves him.
— E. M. FORSTER

Death is also a thought—like life, which is infinite thinking of death.
— EDMOND JABES

The world is impermanent. One should constantly remember death.
— SRI RAMAKRISHNA

The world is a very fine place and worth the fighting for and I hate very much to leave it.
— HEMINGWAY

Life the permission to know death.
— DJUNA BARNES

While I thought I was learning how to live, I have been learning how to die.
— LEONARDO da VINCI

Nobody knows you. You are the neighbor of nothing.
— MARK STRAND

Whom the gods love dies young.
— MENANDER

I see clearly that there are two deaths: to cease loving and being loved is unbearable. But to cease to live is of no consequence.
— VOLTAIRE

Man, like a light in the night, is kindled and put out.
— HERACLITUS

The last act of the comedy is not less beautiful ...
— ANDRE GIDE

The more absurd life is, the more insupportable death is.
— SARTRE

There is...no death...There is only...me...me...who is going to die ...　　　　　　— ANDRE MALRAUX

Death is always swallowed by life.　　　— GOETHE

As death draws near one sees it no more.
　　　　　　　　　　　— RANIER MARIA RILKE

DEFINITION

Every definition is dangerous.　　　— ERASMUS

Definitions might be good things, if only we did not employ words in making them.　　　— ROUSSEAU

To define a thing is to substitute the definition for the thing itself.　　　— GEORGES BRAQUE

DEPARTURES and DESTINATIONS

Set out from any point. They are all alike. They all lead to a point of departure.　　　— ANTONIO PORCHIA

Individuals always did and always do take themselves as points of departure.　　　— KARL MARX

From a certain point onward there is no longer any turning back. That is the point that must be reached.
　　　　　　　　　　　　— KAFKA

Never have I been able to settle in life. Always seated askew, as if on the arm of a chair; ready to get up, to leave.　　　　　　— ANDRE GIDE

Thus we live, for ever taking leave.
— RANIER MARIA RILKE

There is a time for departure even when there's no certain place to go. — TENNESSEE WILLIAMS

And the end of all our exploring will be to arrive where we started and know the place for the first time.
— T. S. ELIOT

Anything we fully do is an alone journey.
— NATALIE GOLDBERG

If you can't go somewhere, move in the passageways of the self. — RUMI

It is good to have an end to journey toward, but it is the journey that matters, in the end. — URSULA K. LeGUIN

Every exit is an entry somewhere else.
— TOM STOPPARD

No man can cut out new paths in company. He does that alone. — OLIVER WENDALL HOLMES

The beauty of independence, departure, actions that rely on themselves. — WALT WHITMAN

DESIRE

Ultimately, one loves one's desires and not that which is desired. — NIETZSCHE

From desire I plunge to its fulfillment, where I long once
more for desire. — GOETHE

Desire is originally desire of being. — SARTRE

DESTRUCTION

Total destruction. In its own way it is a form of ecstasy,
this utter harmony between design and debris. But even
a poet will find it difficult to share this vision on short
notice. — JOHN HAWKES

He who has to be creator always has to destroy.
— NIETZSCHE

Everything that seems to us imperishable tends towards
its destruction. — PROUST

Whoever will be born must destroy a world.
— HERMANN HESSE

A man can be destroyed but not defeated.
— HEMINGWAY

DREAMS and DREAMING

We have no dreams at all or interesting ones. We should
learn to be awake the same way. — NIETZSCHE

As in all dreams the remarkable thing is the vividness
of the reality, the fact that *one is in reality* and not
dreaming. — HENRY MILLER

In dreams begin responsibility.
— WILLIAM BUTLER YEATS

I dream in my dream all the dreams of the other dreamers, / And I become the other dreamers.
— WALT WHITMAN

Dreams are real while they last; can we say more of life?
— HAVELOCK ELLIS

EDUCATION and LEARNING

I learn by going where I have to go.   — ROETHKE

What is really important in education is not that the child learns this and that, but that the mind is matured, that energy is aroused.   — KIERKEGAARD

The great difficulty in education is to get experience out of ideas.   — SANTAYANA

That is what learning is. You suddenly understand something you've understood all your life, but in a new way.
— DORIS LESSING

You have learnt something. That always feels at first as if you had lost something.   — GEORGE BERNARD SHAW

Discovery consists in seeing what everybody has seen and thinking what nobody has thought.
— ALBERT SZENT-GYORGYI

A man only understands what is akin to something already existing in himself. — HENRI FREDERIC AMIEL

Knowledge means: *being able to learn.* — HEIDEGGER

The only real education comes from what goes counter to you. — ANDRE GIDE

Much learning, much sorrow. — JOHN CLARKE

I am still learning.
— MICHAELANGELO, personal motto

EMOTIONS

We choose our joys and sorrows long before we experience them. — KAHLIL GIBRAN

Living, of course, is rather the opposite of expressing.
— CAMUS

To have felt too much is to end in feeling nothing.
— DOROTHY THOMPSON

Emotion is primarily about nothing, and much of it remains about nothing to the end. — SANTAYANA

Like great works, deep feelings always mean more than they are conscious of saying. — CAMUS

We don't have feelings that change us, but feelings that suggest to us the idea of change. — CAMUS

The advantage of emotions is that they lead us astray.
— OSCAR WILDE

EVENTS

You need only to claim the events of your life to make yourself yours. When you truly possess all you have been and done, which may take some time, you are fierce with reality.   — FLORIDA SCOTT-MAXWELL

The greatest events—they are not our loudest but our stillest hours.   — NIETZSCHE

It loved to happen.   — MARCUS AURELIUS

Learn to wish that everything should come to pass as it does.   — EPICTETUS

Great occasions do not make heroes or cowards; they simply unveil them to the eyes of men. Silently and imperceptibly, as we wake or sleep, we grow strong or weak; and at last some crisis shows what we have become.
— BROOKE FOSS WESTCOTT

ETERNITY and TIMELESSNESS

Eternity was in that moment. — WILLIAM CONGREVE

The Indians knew long ago that music was going on permanently and that hearing it was like looking out a window at a landscape which didn't stop when one turned away.   — JOHN CAGE

To see a world in a grain of sand, / And a heaven in a flower; / Hold infinity in the palm of your hand, / And eternity in an hour.　　　　— WILLIAM BLAKE

Eternity scatters the crowd by giving each an infinite weight, by making him heavy—as an individual.
　　　　　　　　　　　　　　— KIERKEGAARD

At bottom the mind conceives man only in the eternal.
　　　　　　　　　　　　　— ANDRE MALRAUX

Eternity is not something that begins after you are dead. It is going on all the time. We are in it now.
　　　　　　　　　　— CHARLOTTE P. GILMAN

To be eternal means to have existed.　　— MAX FRISCH

Eternity is hardly longer than life.　　— RENE CHAR

EXISTENCE and BEING

A is A.　　　　　　　　　　　　— ARISTOTLE

That that is is.　　　　　　　　— SHAKESPEARE

Rose is a rose is a rose is a rose.　— GERTRUDE STEIN

Being is the great explainer.　　　　— THOREAU

Being is what it is.　　　　　　　　— SARTRE

A beautiful soul has no other merit than its own existence.   — J.F.C. von SCHILLER

A fly, when it exists, has as much being as God.
                                        — KIERKEGAARD

Being, not doing, is my first joy.   — ROETHKE

Man is nothing else but that which he makes of himself.
                                              — SARTRE

Existence precedes essence.   — SARTRE

He only earns his freedom and existence who daily conquers them anew.   — GOETHE

Why is there any being at all and rather not Nothing?
                                           — HEIDEGGER

If man, as the existentialist defines him, is indefinable, it is because at first he is nothing.   — SARTRE

Each something is a celebration of the nothing that supports it.   — JOHN CAGE

I stick my finger into existence—it smells of nothing.
                                        — KIERKEGAARD

Being...is not closed for us and the horizons are not finite. On all sides we are impelled towards the infinite.
                                        — KARL JASPERS

Not to be everything, and not to be it forever, is the same as not being at all.   — MIGUEL de UNAMUNO

Existence begins in every instant. — NIETZSCHE

The secret of my universe: just imagine God without man's immortality. — CAMUS

We know that we are ephemeral and that after us there will be nothing worth mentioning.
— BERTOLT BRECHT

At any given moment, I open my eyes and exist. And before that, during all eternity, what was there? Nothing.
— UGO BETTI

As for being and nothingness, the one thing I did know was that to choose between them was simply to choose being, not for the sake of being, or even the love of being, much less the desire to be forever—but in hope of being what I could be for a time. This would be an ecstasy. — WILLIAM STYRON

Existence is a repletion which man can never abandon.
— SARTRE

The being that exists is man. — HEIDEGGER

By being both here and beyond I am becoming a horizon. — MARK STRAND

Being is everywhere. — SARTRE

You do not need to leave your room. Remain sitting at your table and listen. Do not even listen, simply wait. Do not even wait, be quite still and solitary. The world will freely offer itself to you to be unmasked, it has no choice, it will roll in ecstasy at your feet.   — KAFKA

How could there be any question of acquiring or possessing, when the one thing needful for a man is to *become*—to *be* at last, and to die in the fullness of his being.   — SAINT-EXUPERY

There is no having, only being, only a being panting for its last breath, panting to be choked out.   — KAFKA

Must it be? / It must be. — LUDWIG van BEETHOVEN

The sun shone, having no alternative, on the nothing new.   — SAMUEL BECKETT

It is better to be than not to be.
                    — AUCTORITATES ARISTOTELIS

Being has not been given its due.   — SARTRE

EXISTENTIALISM and the ABSURD

The absurd is born of the confrontation between the human call and the unreasonable silence of the world.
                                    — CAMUS

A realistic being does not, as a logical consequence, have to be a non-idealistic being and existentialism can roll itself in dung but likewise bathe in the sea.

— JUAN RAMON JIMENEZ

All of us among the ruins are preparing a renaissance beyond the limits of nihilism.   — CAMUS

Existentialism is a Humanism.   — SARTRE

We are too late for the gods, too early for Being.

— HEIDEGGER

I will agree to be an existentialist as long as I may remain unaware of it.   — ANDRE GIDE

The absurd has meaning only in so far as it is not agreed to.   — CAMUS

We think existentialism is optimistic, a doctrine of action.   — SARTRE

Man is capable of doing what he is incapable of imagining. His head plows through the galaxy of the absurd.

— RENE CHAR

One does not discover the absurd without being tempted to write a manual of happiness.   — CAMUS

Existentialism deals with existence in the manner of a thriller.   — GUIDORE RUGGIERO

Existentialism must be lived to be really sincere. To live as an existentialist means to be ready to pay for this view and not merely lay it down in books. — SARTRE

It is not like sharing in something else, but is at once the understanding and the being of what is understood.
— KARL JASPERS

From the moment absurdity is recognized, it becomes a passion, the most harrowing of all. — CAMUS

EXPERIENCE

Experience is not what happens to you; it is what you do with what happens to you. — ALDOUS HUXLEY

Experience shows us that exceptions are as strong as rules. — EDITH MIRIELLES

Experience teaches only the teachable.
— ALDOUS HUXLEY

The reward of suffering is experience. — AESCHYLUS

Two things reveal the whole of his nature to a man: instinct and experience. — PASCAL

You cannot create experience, you undergo it.
— CAMUS

Men are wise, not in proportion to their experience, but to their capacity for experience.
— GEORGE BERNARD SHAW

In the end one only experiences oneself.
                                    — NIETZSCHE

If you have not lived through something, it is not true.
                                    — KABIR

EXPLANATIONS

I want everything explained to me or nothing.
                                    — CAMUS

I am one of those unfortunates to whom death is less hideous than explanations. — D. B. WYNDHAM LEWIS

Never explain. Your friends do not need it and your enemies will not believe it anyway. — ELBERT HUBBARD

For the absurd man it is not a matter of explaining and solving, but of experiencing and describing. Everything begins with lucid indifference.   — CAMUS

FATE and DESTINY

For man is man and master of his fate.
                                    — ALFRED, LORD TENNYSON

Every man is the architect of his own fortune.
                                    — APPIUS CLAUDIUS CAECUS

And when man faces destiny, destiny ends and man comes into his own.   — ANDRE MALRAUX

Human reason needs only to will more strongly than fate, and she *is* fate. — THOMAS MANN

I want to seize fate by the throat.

— LUDWIG van BEETHOVEN

I have anticipated you, Fortune, and have barred your means of entry. — EPICURUS

By the side of fate, set up resistance to fate. You will know strange heights. — RENE CHAR

What you call chance—you yourself are that which befalls and astonishes you. — NIETZSCHE

None but yourself shall you meet on the highway of fate.
— MAURICE MAETERLINCK

All that remains is a fate whose outcome alone is fatal.
— CAMUS

A man's character is his fate. — HERACLITUS

Fate keeps on happening. — ANITA LOOS

I do not believe in a fate that falls on men however they act; but I do believe in a fate that falls on them unless they act. — G. K. CHESTERTON

Coincidence, if traced back far enough, becomes inevitable. — HINEU

There is no more chance. — NIETZSCHE

They...who await no gifts from Chance, have conquered Fate. — MATTHEW ARNOLD

We are not permitted to choose the frame of our destiny. But what we put into it is ours.
— DAG HAMMARSKJOLD

A wise man builds his own destiny. — PLAUTUS

There is no fate that cannot be surmounted by scorn.
— CAMUS

The torment of precaution often exceeds the dangers to be avoided. It is sometimes better to abandon one's self to destiny. — NAPOLEON I

Intellect annuls fate. — EMERSON

I know my fate. — NIETZSCHE

I feel that I am the man of destiny.
— J.F.C. von SCHILLER

That's what Destiny means: being face to face, / and nothing else, and always face to face.
— RANIER MARIA RILKE

FEAR

It is fear that first brought gods into the world.
— PETRONIUS

We must travel in the direction of our fear.
— JOHN BERRYMAN

Nothing in life is to be feared. It is only to be understood.
— MARIE CURIE

His fear did not seek to become a god.
— JEAN COCTEAU

Once men are caught up in an event they cease to be afraid. Only the unknown frightens men.
— SAINT-EXUPERY

Courage is resistance to fear, mastery of fear—not absence of fear. — MARK TWAIN

Fear is the main source of superstition and one of the main sources of cruelty. To conquer fear is the beginning of wisdom. — BERTRAND RUSSELL

One can only be afraid of life. — OTTO WEININGER

FORGIVING

And if your friend does evil to you, say to him, "I forgive you for what you did to me, but how can I forgive you for what you did to yourself?" — NIETZSCHE

How do you do it is nice to meet you I forgive you everything and there is nothing to forgive.
— GERTRUDE STEIN

FREEDOM

Freedom is the will to be responsible to ourselves.
— NIETZSCHE

You are free and that is why you are lost. — KAFKA

Man is condemned to be free. — SARTRE

Men are only free when they are doing what their deepest self likes...it takes some diving.
— D. H. LAWRENCE

He who does not enjoy solitude will not love freedom.
— ARTHUR SCHOPENHAUER

Free but alone. — JOSEPH JOACHIM, personal motto

Freedom is...a long-distance race, quite solitary and very exhausting. — CAMUS

I am free when I am within myself. — HEGEL

I wish that every human life might be pure transparent freedom. — SIMONE de BEAUVOIR

Freedom is not procured by a full enjoyment of what is desired, but by controlling the desire. — EPICTETUS

If man didn't sometimes *sovereignly* close his eyes, he would end up no longer seeing what is worth being looked at. — RENE CHAR

Let us leave every man at liberty to seek into himself and to lose himself in his own ideas. — VOLTAIRE

Human existence and freedom are from the beginning inseparable. — ERICH FROMM

Man is free. The coward makes himself cowardly. The hero makes himself heroic. — SARTRE

It is in freedom that the inward activity of all life is made perceptible. — NICOLAS BERDYAEV

I *am* my freedom. — SARTRE

Freedom is what you do with what's been done to you. — SARTRE

The free man is a warrior. — NIETZSCHE

Once freedom lights its beacon in a man's heart, the gods are powerless against him. — SARTRE

FRIENDS and FRIENDSHIP

Friends are born, not made. — HENRY ADAMS

A friend is, as it were, a second self. — CICERO

Friendship needs no words—it is solitude delivered from the anguish of loneliness. — DAG HAMMARSKJOLD

The friendships that last are those wherein each friend respects the other's dignity to the point of not really wanting anything from him. — CYRIL CONNOLLY

If you press me to say why I loved him, I can say no more than it was because he was he, and I was I. — MONTAIGNE

Each friend represents a world in us, a world possibly not born until they arrive, and it is only by this meeting that a new world is born. — ANAIS NIN

We need new friends. Some of us are cannibals who have eaten their old friends up; others must have ever-renewed audiences before whom to reenact an ideal version of their lives. — LOGAN PAERSALL SMITH

How could sincerity be a condition of friendship? A taste for the truth at any cost is a passion which spares nothing. — CAMUS

A friend should be a master at guessing and keeping still. — NIETZSCHE

Of my friends I am the only one I have left. — TERENCE

And if I speak of an art of friendship, it is of an art that leaves man free... — JEAN COCTEAU

The FUTURE

We must keep in mind that the future is neither completely ours nor not ours, so that we should not fully expect it to come, nor lose hope, as if it were not coming at all. — EPICURUS

Never let the future disturb you. You will meet it, if you have to, with the same weapons of reason which today arm you against the present. — MARCUS AURELIUS

The future is no more uncertain than the present.
— WALT WHITMAN

The future stands firm, my dear Mr. Kappas, but we move in infinite space.
— RANIER MARIA RILKE

The future influences the present just as much as the past.
— NIETZSCHE

Madame, there are always two paths to take; one back towards the comforts and security of death, the other forward to nowhere.
— HENRY MILLER

Life is an operation which is done in a forward direction.
— JOSE ORTEGA Y GASSETT

The future is not in the past; it is in the future.
— JEAN GUITTON

GENERALIZATIONS

All generalizations are false, including this one.
— ALEXANDER CHASE

GENIUS

It takes a lot of time to be a genius, you have to sit around so much doing nothing, really doing nothing.
— GERTRUDE STEIN

There is a certain characteristic common to all those
whom we call geniuses. Each of them has a consciousness of being a man apart. — MIGUEL de UNAMUNO

GIFTS and GIVING

The only gift is a portion of thyself. — EMERSON

I know what I have given you. I do not know what you
have received. — ANTONIO PORCHIA

GOODBYES and PARTING

It is never any good dwelling on goodbyes. It is not the
being together that it prolongs, it is the parting.
— ELIZABETH BIBESCO

Not how one soul comes close to another but how it
moves away shows me their kinship and how much they
belong together. — NIETZSCHE

I leave. / You stay. / Two autumns. — BUSON

In every parting there is the image of death.
— GEORGE ELIOT

It is worthwhile falling in love, if only for the parting.
— JULIUSZ SKOWACKI

"Farewell," says the dying man to his reflection in the
mirror that is held up to him, "we shall not meet again."
— VALERY

GREATNESS

He only is a great man who can neglect the applause of the multitude and enjoy himself independent of its favour.   — JOSEPH ADDISON

It is when we pass our own private gate, and open our own secret door, that we step into the land of the giants.
                                                                              — G. K. CHESTERTON

The struggle itself toward the heights is enough to fill a man's heart. One must imagine Sisyphus happy.
                                                                              — CAMUS

Of what is great one must either be silent or speak with greatness.   — NIETZSCHE

Anything may be betrayed. Anything may be forgiven. But not those who lack the courage of their own greatness.   — AYN RAND

Greatness is possible, but exceptional, at all times.
                                                                              — WALTER KAUFMANN

To be great is to be misunderstood.   — EMERSON

Greatness knows itself.   — SHAKESPEARE

Great men can't be ruled.   — AYN RAND

There is a melancholy that stems from greatness of mind.
                                                                              — CHAMFORT

Every great man is a unique.   — EMERSON

HABIT

The evolution from happiness to habit is one of death's best weapons.   — JULIO CORTAZAR

Habit is the great deadener.   — SAMUEL BECKETT

To fall into habit is to cease to be.
          — MIGUEL de UNAMUNO

HAPPINESS

Happiness depends upon ourselves.   — ARISTOTLE

To be happy, we must not be too concerned with others.
          — CAMUS

I believe in the possibility of happiness, if one cultivates intuition and outlives the grosser passions, including optimism.   — SANTAYANA

The secret of happiness is to face the fact that the world is horrible, horrible, horrible...you must feel it deeply and not brush it aside.   — BERTRAND RUSSELL

Happiness and the absurd are two sons of the same earth. They are inseparable.   — CAMUS

We must, therefore, pursue the things that make for happiness, given that when happiness is present, we have everything; but when it is absent, we do everything to possess it.   — EPICURUS

Be happy. It is one way of being wise. — COLETTE

Happiness is the moment we don't want to trade in for not-being. — BARON de MONTESQUIEU

If you want to be happy, be. — LEO TOLSTOY

Immediacy is happiness, because in immediacy there is no contradiction. — KIERKEGAARD

The only happiness worth the name is the natural happiness of conscious being. — NISARGADATTA MAHARAJ

For what end is served by all the expenditure of suns and planets and moons, of stars and Milky Ways, of comets and nebula, of worlds evolving and passing away, if at last a happy man does not involuntarily rejoice in his existence? — NIETZSCHE

Happiness is the only sanction of life; where happiness fails, existence remains a sad and lamentable experiment. — SANTAYANA

Happiness is light on the water. The water is cold and dark and deep. — WILLIAM MAXWELL

The happy man is he who knows his limitations, yet bows to no false gods. — ROBERT SERVICE

Happy the man, and happy he alone, / He who can call today his own; / He who secure within can say, / Tomorrow do thy worst, for I have lived today.
— JOHN DRYDEN

The will of man is his happiness.

— J.F.C. von SCHILLER

Not to call a thing good a day longer or a day sooner than it seems good to us is the only way to remain really happy.   — NIETZSCHE

To increase the happiness of a man's life is to extend the tragic nature of the witness he bears.   — CAMUS

Happiness makes up in height for what it lacks in length.

— ROBERT FROST

To fill the hour—that is happiness.   — EMERSON

Happiness lies in the consciousness we have of it.

— GEORGE SAND

Nothing is more fatal to happiness than the remembrance of happiness.   — ANDRE GIDE

Happiness is essentially a state of going somewhere, wholeheartedly, one-directionally, without regret or reservation.   — WILLIAM H. SHELDON

Remember that happiness is a way of travel—not a destination.   — ROY GOODMAN

It is not easy to find happiness in ourselves, and it is not possible to find it elsewhere.   — AGNES REPPLIER

Man is the artificer of his own happiness. — THOREAU

What interests me isn't the happiness of every man, but that of each man. — BORIS VIAN

Anything you're good at contributes to happiness.
— BERTRAND RUSSELL

By the grace of reality and the nature of life, man— every man—is an end in himself, he exists for his own sake, and the achievement of his happiness is his highest moral purpose. — AYN RAND

There is no duty we so much underrate as the duty of being happy. — ROBERT LOUIS STEVENSON

Happiness is not the reward of virtue, but is virtue itself.
— SPINOZA

The good, as I conceive it, is happiness, happiness for each man after his own heart, and for each hour according to its inspiration. — SANTAYANA

HEALTH

Give me health and a day, and I will make the pomp of emperors ridiculous. — EMERSON

Use your health, even to the point of wearing it out. That is what it is there for. Spend all you have before you die, and do not outlive yourself.
— GEORGE BERNARD SHAW

Purer and more honest of speech is the healthy body, perfect and square-built: and it speaks of the meaning of the earth. — NIETZSCHE

HELL

What is hell? I maintain that it is the suffering of being unable to love. — DOSTOEVSKY

Hell is more bearable than nothingness. — P.J. BAILEY

Hell is truth seen too late. — UNKNOWN

Hell is other people. — SARTRE

HISTORY

History, with all her volumes vast, / Hath but one page. — LORD BYRON

Every man is a history of the world for himself. — MAX STIRNER

History explains neither the natural universe which came before it, nor beauty which stands above it. — CAMUS

Excess of history harms the living. — NIETZSCHE

Happy the people whose annals are blank. — THOMAS CARLYLE

There is properly no history; only biography. — EMERSON

Every age has conditions of its own and is an individual situation; decisions must and can be made only within...the age itself. In the turmoil of world affairs, no universal principle, no memory of similar conditions in the past can help us—a vague memory has no power against the vitality and freedom of the moment.

— HEGEL

IDEAL

We need never regard the ideal as distant or nonexistent because the ideal is in ourselves.

— JUAN RAMON JIMENEZ

He who attains his ideal by that very fact transcends it.

— NIETZSCHE

The ideal is in thyself, the impediment too is in thyself.

— THOMAS CARLYLE

No man can set up an ideal for another, nor labor to realize it for him.

— SANTAYANA

IDEAS

If you are possessed by an idea, you find it expressed everywhere, you even smell it.

— THOMAS MANN

An idea is not so powerless that it cannot make itself into more than an idea.

— HEGEL

Ideas are substitutes for griefs.

— PROUST

The world is my idea. — SCHOPENHAUER

IDENTITY

Man is nothing else but that which he makes of himself.
— SARTRE

One can lose everything, as long as one remains what one is. — GOETHE

None but himself can be his parallel.
— LEWIS THEOBALD

He steps into the mirror, refusing to be anyone else.
— FRANK O'HARA

I imitate everyone except myself. — PICASSO

I am a part of all that I have met.
— ALFRED, LORD TENNYSON

Become what you are. — PINDAR

IMAGINATION

listen: there's a hell of a good universe next door: let's go!
— e. e. cummings

Imagined life is more exhilarating than remembered life.
— JOHN HAWKES

I like a view but I like to sit with my back turned to it.
— GERTRUDE STEIN

I admit that twice two makes four is an excellent thing, but if we are to give everything its due, twice two makes five is sometimes a very charming thing too.
— DOSTOEVSKY

IMMORTALITY

Love of life is almost the opposite of love of long life.
— NIETZSCHE

Millions long for immortality who do not know what to do with themselves on a rainy Sunday afternoon.
— SUSAN ERTZ

Stavrogin: "Do you believe in eternal life in the other world?"
Kirilov: "No, but in eternal life in this world."
— DOSTOEVSKY

Immortality is an idea with no future.   — CAMUS

Being and immortality are the same. — KARL JASPERS

What matters is not eternal life but eternal vivacity.
— NIETZSCHE

He had decided to live forever or die in the attempt.
— JOSEPH HELLER

INDIVIDUALISM

to be nobody but yourself—in a world which is doing its best, night and day, to make you everybody else—means to fight the hardest battle which any human being can fight, and never stop fighting. — e. e. cummings

Individualism is in one sense the only possible ideal.
— SANTAYANA

For there is nothing that pleases me more than that I should always be the way I am and they the way they are. — JULIUS CAESAR

From childhood's hour I have not been / As others were— I have not seen / As others saw.
— EDGAR ALLEN POE

In this world we have to burn completely, resolve ourselves fully, each one in the flames and the resolution appropriate to him. — JUAN RAMON JIMENEZ

When two do the same thing, it is not the same thing at all. — PUBLIUS SYRUS

The singular is not particular; it is universal.
— MIGUEL de UNAMUNO

My great mistake, the fault for which I can't forgive myself, is that one day I ceased my obstinate pursuit of my own individuality. — OSCAR WILDE

And yet, if I were to design an inscription for my tombstone, I should desire none other than "That Individual."
— KIERKEGAARD

Be a man and do not follow me—but yourself.
— NIETZSCHE

The INEXPRESSIBLE

If man is to regain once more...proximity with Being, then he must learn first of all to exist in the nameless.
— HEIDEGGER

Not all of the most simple and important things have a name.
— PAUL VALERY

There are thousands of ideas that are impossible to translate into popular language.
— ROUSSEAU

I wrote of silences, of nights, I expressed the inexpressible...I took hold of the heights.
— RIMBAUD

I see myself lying in my little crib, not sleeping, and somehow foreseeing that life would be this way: full of special things which are meant for *one* only and which are unutterable.
— RANIER MARIA RILKE

After silence, that which comes nearest to expressing the inexpressible is music.
— ALDOUS HUXLEY

Human life is driven forward by its dim apprehension of notions too general for its existing language.
— ALFRED NORTH WHITEHEAD

Explanation of the unspeakable cannot be finished.

— BUDDHA

INFLUENCE

People exercise an unconscious selection in being influenced.

— T. S. ELIOT

Influence is neither good nor bad in an absolute manner, but only in relation to the one who experiences it.

— ANDRE GIDE

INNOCENCE

The innocent is the person who explains nothing.

— CAMUS

Experience, which destroys innocence, also leads one back to it.

— JAMES BALDWIN

INSIGHT

A moment's insight is sometimes worth a life's experience.

— OLIVER WENDALL HOLMES

To see clearly is poetry, prophecy, and religion—all in one.

— JOHN RUSKIN

INSPIRATION

We should refer, not to inspiration, but to expiration. That which we call inspiration comes from ourselves, from within our own night. — JEAN COCTEAU

Joys impregnate. Sorrows bring forth.
— WILLIAM BLAKE

INTELLIGENCE and INTELLECT

An intellectual is someone whose mind watches itself.
— CAMUS

Intelligence is quickness in seeing things as they are.
— SANTAYANA

The greatest intelligence is precisely the one that suffers the most from its own limitations. — GIDE

INTROSPECTION

There is only one great adventure and that is inwards towards the self. — HENRY MILLER

To enter one's own self, it is necessary to go armed to the teeth. — PAUL VALERY

Who's not sat tense before his own heart's curtain?
— RANIER MARIA RILKE

The unexamined life is not worth living. — ARISTOTLE

Whoever looks into himself as into vast space and carries galaxies in himself also knows how irregular all galaxies are; they lead into the chaos and labyrinth of existence. — NIETZSCHE

KNOWLEDGE

It was the greatest sensation of existence, not to trust, but to know. — AYN RAND

To know is not to prove, nor to explain. It is to accede to vision. — SAINT-EXUPERY

True knowledge is not attained by thinking. It is what you are; it is what you become. — SRI AUROBINDO

We are being torn apart between the avidity for knowing and the despair of having known. — RENE CHAR

I want to know if I can live with what I know, and that only. — CAMUS

I know all one can know when one knows nothing. — MARGUERITE DURAS

Knowledge is recognition of something absent; it is a salutation, not an embrace. — SANTAYANA

Today people despair of true knowledge. — CAMUS

To know that we know what we know, and that we do not know what we do not know, that is true knowledge.

— THOREAU

The things we know best are the things we haven't been taught.
— VAUVENARGUES

All knowledge is *interpretation.*
— KARL JASPERS

There is only knowledge from a point of view.

— SARTRE

I have tried to know absolutely nothing about a great many things, and I have succeeded fairly well.
— ROBERT BENCHLY

The only pleasure is to rediscover for oneself the whole of knowledge.
— MICHEL SERVIN

If I only had the courage to think all that I know.
— NIETZSCHE

Knowledge is its own price.
— JEAN de la FONTAINE

Without knowledge, life is no more than the shadow of death.
— MOLIERE

One no longer loves one's knowledge when one has communicated it.
— NIETZSCHE

All men desire by nature to know.
— ARISTOTLE

LIES and LYING

I am a lie that always tells the truth. — JEAN COCTEAU

There is a truth in the activities of the deceiver.

— SARTRE

The most common sort of lie is that by which a man deceives himself: the deception of others is a relatively rare offense. — NIETZSCHE

The lie is a condition of life. — NIETZSCHE

LIFE and LIVING

Life is a cluster of disappointments made bearable by the challenges they establish. — PETER VANSITTART

Life is a horizontal fall. — JEAN COCTEAU

There is no meaning to life except the meaning man gives his life by the unfolding of his powers.

— ERICH FROMM

Life has a meaning if we choose to give it one.

— SARTRE

The aim of living is life itself. — GOETHE

The meaning of life is that it stops. — KAFKA

All actual life is encounter. — MARTIN BUBER

Life is like nothing, because it is everything.
— WILLIAM GOLDING

Man must live and create—live to the point of tears.
— CAMUS

Living well and beautifully and justly are all one thing.
— SOCRATES

The days come and go like muffled and veiled figures sent from a distant friendly party, but they say nothing, and if we do not use the gifts they bring, they carry them as silently away.
— EMERSON

You only live once—but if you work it right, once is enough.
— JOE E. LEWIS

Thou shalt love life more than the meaning of life.
— DOSTOEVSKY, personal maxim.

See into life—don't just look at it.
— ANNE BAXTER

People living deeply do not fear death.
— ANAIS NIN

The mystery of life is not a problem to be solved but a reality to be experienced.
— AART van der LEEUW

Life has the name of life, but in reality it is death.
— HERACLITUS

There is one reason why we cannot complain of life: it keeps no one against his will.
— SENECA

One must choose in life between boredom and torment.
— GERMAINE de STAEL

The truth is that life is delicious, horrible, charming, frightful, sweet, bitter, and that it is everything.
— ANATOLE FRANCE

Life's but a walking shadow, a poor player / That struts and frets his hour upon the stage / And then is heard no more: it is a tale / Told by an idiot, full of sound and fury, signifying nothing.
— SHAKESPEARE

Life is battle and a sojourn in a strange land, and the fame that comes after is oblivion.
— MARCUS AURELIUS

It is enough.
— IMMANUEL KANT, last words

The idea of life having a purpose stands and falls with the religious system.
— SIGMUND FREUD

Life and love are life and love, a bunch of violets is a bunch of violets, and to drag in the idea of a point is to ruin everything. Live and let live, love and let love, flower and fade, and follow the natural curve, which flows on, pointless.
— D.H. LAWRENCE

Where I am, I don't know, I'll never know, in the silence you don't know, you must go on, I can't go on, I'll go on.
— SAMUEL BECKETT

Living is keeping the absurd alive.
— CAMUS

Every day look at a beautiful picture, read a beautiful poem, listen to some beautiful music, and if possible, say some reasonable thing. — GOETHE

Every man must look to himself to teach him the meaning of life. It is not something discovered; it is something moulded. — SAINT-EXUPERY

In life, a man commits himself, draws his own portrait and there is nothing but that portrait. — SARTRE

If we have our own "why" in life, we shall get along with almost any "how." — NIETZSCHE

Life has to be given meaning because of the obvious fact that it has no meaning. — HENRY MILLER

Life is the art of drawing sufficient conclusions from insufficient premises. — SAMUEL BUTLER

To be what we are, and to become what we are capable of becoming, is the only end in life. — ROBERT LOUIS STEVENSON

The problem is not life after death, which I regard as absurd, but life before death. That is urgent, real and earnest. — HUGH CUDLIPP

That life is worth living is the most necessary of assumptions, and, were it not assumed, the most impossible of conclusions. — SANTAYANA

There is no cure for birth and death, save to enjoy the interval. — SANTAYANA

Life is a stranger's sojourn, a night at an inn.

— MARCUS AURELIUS

Let us live while we live.   — PHILIP DODDRIDGE

To live is to verify.   — CAMUS

Life, well spent, is long.   — LEONARDO da VINCI

No single event can awaken within us a stranger totally unknown to us. To live is to slowly be born.

— SAINT-EXUPERY

To live is to be born every minute. Death occurs when life stops.   — ERICH FROMM

All of life is more or less what the French would call *s'imposer*—to be able to create one's own terms for what one does.   — KENNETH TYNAN

To live is, in itself, a value judgement. To breathe is to judge.   — CAMUS

Life consists in what a man is thinking of all day.

— EMERSON

Life is what comes next. — JOSE ORTEGA Y GASSETT

Man is abandoned on earth in the midst of his infinite responsibilities, without help, with no aim but what he sets himself.   — SARTRE

There is just one life for each of us—our own.

— EURIPEDES

There are two things to aim at in life: first, to get what you want; and, after that, to enjoy it. Only the wisest of mankind achieve the second.

— LOGAN PEARSALL SMITH

May you live all the days of your life.

— JONATHAN SWIFT

A being who does not hold his own life as the motive and goal of his actions is acting on the motive and standard of death. — AYN RAND

I shall tell you a great secret, my friend. Don't wait for the Last Judgement. It takes place every day. — CAMUS

I wish that life should not be cheap, but sacred. I wish the days to be as centuries, loaded, fragrant.

— EMERSON

I do not cut my life up into days but my days into lives, each day, each hour, an entire life.

— JUAN RAMON JIMENEZ

The most beautiful music is the music of what happens.

— IRISH PROVERB

Eternal childhood. Life calls again. — KAFKA

LONELINESS

Loneliness is and always has been the central and inevitable experience of every man. — THOMAS WOLFE

Language has created the word "loneliness" to express the pain of being alone, and the word "solitude" to express the glory of being alone. — PAUL TILLICH

At the innermost core of all loneliness is a deep and powerful yearning for union with one's lost self.
— BRENDAN FRANCIS

What makes a man feel alone is the cowardice of others.
— CAMUS

To one man, lonesomeness is the flight of the sick one; to another, it is the flight *from* the sick ones.
— NIETZSCHE

Man's loneliness is but his fear of life.
— EUGENE O'NEILL

LOVE

It is true: we love life, not because we are used to living but because we are used to loving. — NIETZSCHE

I know of only one duty, and that is to love. — CAMUS

I love, therefore I exist. — DOSTOEVSKY

Everywhere, we learn only from those we love.
— GOETHE

When one loves somebody, everything is clear—where to go, what to do—it all takes care of itself and one doesn't have to ask anybody about anything. — MAXIM GORKY

Love is always life—and only life. / There is no gaze of love that does not give birth to / its eternity.
— JORGE GUILLEN

In love the paradox occurs that two beings become one and yet remain two. — ERICH FROMM

Life has taught us that love does not consist in gazing at one another but in looking outward together in the same direction. — SAINT-EXUPERY

Sometimes it is a form of love just to talk to somebody that you have nothing in common with and still be fascinated by their presence. — DAVID BYRNE

Words are the weak support of cold indifference; love has no language to be heard. — WILLIAM CONGREVE

They do not love who do not show their love.
— SHAKESPEARE

What I cannot love, I overlook. — ANAIS NIN

The lover is a monotheist who knows other people worship different gods but cannot himself imagine their presence. — THEODOR REIK

The story of love is not important—what is important is that one is capable of love. It is perhaps the only glimpse we are permitted of eternity.   — HELEN HAYES

O, tell her, brief is life but love is long.
                    — ALFRED, LORD TENNYSON

None love, but those who wish to love.   — RACINE

In the act of loving someone you arm them against you.
                    — UNKNOWN

Love is, above all, the gift of oneself. — JEAN ANOUILH

This is the hardest of all: to close the open hand out of love, and remain modest as a giver.   — NIETZSCHE

Genuine love is nothing but the attempt to exchange two solitudes.   — JOSE ORTEGA Y GASSETT

There is this to be said for the Happy Ending: that the healthy man goes from love to love.
                    — F. SCOTT FITZGERALD

Love is love when it gives pleasure.
                    — WALTHER von der VOGELWEIDE

Happiness comes more from loving than being loved; and often when one affection seems wounded it is only our vanity bleeding. To love, and to be hurt often, and to love again—this is the brave and happy life.
                    — J. E. BUCKROSE

Love is the true price of love.   — GEORGE HERBERT

I love you as you are, but do not tell me how that is.
                                        — ANTONIO PORCHIA

There can be no peace of mind in love, since the advantage one has secured is never anything but a fresh starting point for further desires.   — MARCEL PROUST

If you love me, / Be happy for ever!   — GOETHE

I love you so much that nothing can matter to me—not even you.   — AYN RAND

Love consists in this, that two solitudes protect and touch and greet each other.   — RANIER MARIA RILKE

After all, my erstwhile dear, / My no longer cherished, / Need we say it was no love, / Just because it perished?
                              — EDNA ST. VINCENT MILLAY

Whatever is done for love occurs beyond good and evil.
                                        — NIETZSCHE

Who ever loved, that loved not at first sight?
                              — CHRISTOPHER MARLOWE

With love one can live even without happiness.
                                        — DOSTOEVSKY

To fall in love is to create a religion with a fallible god.
                              — JORGE LUIS BORGES

When two people love each other there can be no happy
end to it.   — HEMINGWAY

Love is more afraid of change than destruction.
                                       — NIETZSCHE

Only by oneself, apart, can one consummate this seem-
ingly most shared experience that love is.
                            — RANIER MARIA RILKE

There is no noble love save that which recognizes itself
to be both short-lived and exceptional.   — CAMUS

LUCK

It is a great piece of skill to know how to guide your luck
even while waiting for it.   — BALTASAR GRACIAN

MAN

Man is Man.   — AYN RAND

The belly of being does not speak to man, except as man.
                                       — NIETZSCHE

Man be my metaphor.   — DYLAN THOMAS

Man simply is.   — SARTRE

Every man is to be regarded as an absolute end in
himself.   — IMMANUEL KANT

To be a man is, precisely, to be responsible.

— SAINT-EXUPERY

How proud the word rings—Man!   — MAXIM GORKI

In the nineteenth century the problem was that God is dead; in the twentieth century the problem is that man is dead.   — ERICH FROMM

Man can paint, or make, or think nothing but man.

— EMERSON

You say in big strident tones: *I am a man*...That is enough...If it were possible you would like to go on saying *I am a man* ad lib in order to hide the more terrible stage whisper *I am an artist* and from there to the ultimate blinding conclusion *I am God* !!

— LAWRENCE DURRELL

Here I sit, forming mankind / In my own image / A race resembling me.   — GOETHE

In choosing myself, I choose man.   — SARTRE

The greatest saving you can make...is to accept the unintelligibility of the world—and pay attention to man.
— CAMUS

But neither politics nor ethics nor philosophy is an end in itself, neither in life or in literature. Only Man is an end in himself.   — AYN RAND

Man, in a way, is everything.   — KARL JASPERS

Man is the future of man. — FRANCIS PONGE

Wonders are many, and none is more wonderful than Man. — SOPHOCLES

Man is the keeper of being. — HEIDEGGER

The more you feel you are a human being, / The more you resemble the gods! — GOETHE

A man is a god in ruins. — EMERSON

Man is the great poet. — THOREAU

Man is a part of Nature, not something to be contrasted with Nature. — BERTRAND RUSSELL

Man is the measure of all things. — PROTAGORUS

MAN vs. SOCIETY

There is no way you can benefit society more than by becoming the metal that you know is yourself.
— HENRIK IBSEN

O how contemptible a thing is man unless he can rise himself above humanity. — SENECA

The individual tries to escape the race. And as soon as he ceases to represent the race, he represents man.
— ANDRE GIDE

Once conform, once do what others do because they do it, and a kind of lethargy steals over all the finer senses of the soul.   — MONTAIGNE

You just have to be afraid of men and of them alone.
     — CELINE

Whatever you can provide yourself with to secure your protection from men is a natural good.   — EPICURUS

All that which proceeds from man's independent ego is good. All that which proceeds from man's dependence upon men is evil.   — AYN RAND

I like man, but not men.   — EMERSON

The time when, most of all, you should withdraw into yourself is when you are forced to be in a crowd.
     — EPICURUS

The great problem of life is knowing how to slip between men.   — CAMUS

Whosoever would be a man must be a nonconformist.
     — EMERSON

The crowd is untruth.   — KIERKEGAARD

Society everywhere is in conspiracy against the manhood of every one of its members.   — EMERSON

I teach you the Superman. Man is something that should be overcome.   — NIETZSCHE

MEMORY

My memory is never so happy as when I ignore it.
— JEAN COCTEAU

I have a wonderful memory; I forget everything. It is wonderfully convenient. It is as though the world were constantly renewing itself for me.   — JULES RENARD

Many a man fails to become a great thinker because his memory is too good.   — NIETZSCHE

Memories are killing.   — SAMUEL BECKETT

A memory is what is left when something happens and does not completely unhappen.   — EDWARD de BONO

The advantage of a bad memory is that one enjoys several times the same good thing for the first time.
— NIETZSCHE

To want to forget something is to think of it.
— FRENCH PROVERB

Not the power to remember, but its very opposite, the power to forget, is a necessary condition of our existence.   — SHOLEM ASCH

The MINORITY

Every step of progress the world has made has been from scaffold to scaffold, and stake to stake.
— WENDELL PHILLIPS

Few sometimes may know, when thousands err.
— JOHN MILTON

The world will be saved by the few.   — ANDRE GIDE

The minority is always right.   — HENRIK IBSEN

The MOMENT

Each moment presents what happens.   — JOHN CAGE

Each moment is a place you've never been.
— MARK STRAND

Every minute of life carries with it its miraculous value, and its face of eternal youth.   — CAMUS

Seize from every moment its unique novelty and do not prepare your joys.   — ANDRE GIDE

Right now a moment of time is passing by!...We must become that moment.   — CEZANNE

I have the happiness of the passing moment, and what more can mortal ask?   — GEORGE GISSING

He who seizes the right moment, / Is the right man.
— GOETHE

Carpe dieum. (Seize the day.)   — LATIN PROVERB

What is actual is actual for only one time. / And for only one place.   — T. S. ELIOT

The moment is like a song rising from a dream and we are its heroes. — JUAN RAMON JIMENEZ

The summer moon hung full in the sky. For the time being it was the great fact of the world.
— WILLA CATHER

My candle burns at both ends / It will not last the night / But oh, my foes and ah, my friends / it gives a lovely light! — EDNA ST. VINCENT MILLAY

Gather ye rosebuds while ye may, / Old time is still a-flying, / And this same flower that smiles today / Tomorrow will be dying. — ROBERT HERRICK

Nothing in life is certain for men, children of a day.
— UNKNOWN

Every situation—nay, every moment—is of infinite worth; for it is representative of a whole eternity.
— GOETHE

Now and always. — ITALIAN EXPRESSION

I realized that I never had the least interest in living, but only in this which I am doing right now, something which is parallel to life, of it at the same time, and beyond it.
— HENRY MILLER

Remember that the sole life which a man can lose is that which he is living at the moment.
— MARCUS AURELIUS

And if there is not any such thing as a long time, nor the rest of your lives, nor from now on, but there is only now, why then now is the thing to praise and I am very happy with it.   — HEMINGWAY

Each second is a universe of time.   — HENRY MILLER

We do not remember days, we remember moments.
                                              — CESARE PAVASE

The moment is the sole reality.   — KARL JASPERS

Only the moment counts. It determines life. — KAFKA

MORALS and MORALITY

The morality that would un-self man is the morality of decline.   — NIETZSCHE

We live for something which goes farther than morality.
                                                  — CAMUS

To be moral is to discover fundamentally one's own being.   — SIMONE de BEAUVOIR

The purpose of morality is to teach you, not to suffer and to die, but to enjoy yourself and live.   — AYN RAND

I only know that what is right is what you feel good after and what is immoral is what you feel bad after.
                                              — HEMINGWAY

Waste no more time arguing what a good man should be. Be one. — MARCUS AURELIUS

There is nothing either good or bad but thinking makes it so. — SHAKESPEARE

True morality mocks at morals. — PASCAL

The root of all morality is self-control. — FICHTE

To fail to be human would mean to slip into nothingness. — KARL JASPERS

Morality which is based on ideas, or an ideal, is an unmitigated evil. — D.H. LAWRENCE

Morality is the herd instinct in the individual. — NIETZSCHE

Our moral problem is man's indifference to himself. — ERICH FROMM

The ethical is the universal, and only when the individual becomes the universal is it possible to realize the ethical. — KIERKEGAARD

The moral choice is comparable to the construction of a work of art. — SARTRE

There is no such thing in a man's nature as a settled and full resolve either for good or evil, except at the very moment of execution. — NATHANIEL HAWTHORNE

The highest possible stage in moral culture is when we recognize that we ought to control our thoughts.

— CHARLES DARWIN

My demand upon the philosopher is known, that he takes his stand *beyond* good and evil and leave the illusion of moral judgement *beneath* himself.   — NIETZSCHE

Out beyond fields of wrongdoing and rightdoing, there is a field. I will meet you there.   — RUMI

Nature knows no indecencies; Man invents them.

— MARK TWAIN

The only man who desires to be moral is the man who desires to live.   — AYN RAND

NAMES

In order to live we must have a name; but in order to enter the world of writing we must, along with our name, accept the hazard of every sound, every symbol that perpetuates it.   — EDMOND JABES

To perpetuate one's name, one must carve it on a heavy stone and sink it to the bottom of the sea; depths last longer than heights.   — HERMAN MELVILLE

He stood as if he were looking at the sound of his name in his room. He had all he had wanted.   — AYN RAND

Have all the keys removed from your typewriter except the ones needed to spell her name.   — UNKNOWN

Let us not give them a name…they may have had so many other adventures.   — ALAIN ROBBE-GRILLET

Read my lips, forget my name. — WILLIAM STAFFORD

You would find it ridiculous if, when you asked someone his name, he replied, "My name is whatever you like to call it." You would find such an answer ridiculous. And if he were to add, "I have whatever name you care to give me, and that is my real name," you would consider him mad. And yet that is what we must perhaps get accustomed to; indeterminacy become a positive fact, a positive element of knowledge.   — PAUL VALERY

Another way of approaching the thing is to consider it unnamed, unnameable.   — FRANCIS PONGE

I confused things with their names: that is belief.
                                                     — SARTRE

NATURE

Everything in nature is separate.— GERMAN PROVERB

The unnatural—that too is natural.   — GOETHE

Nature is the principle of movement of it own accord.
                                                     — BOETHIUS

Nature is visible thought.   — HEINRICH HEINE

To make progress in understanding there is only nature.
— CEZANNE

Every individual is an expression of the whole realm of nature, a unique action of the total universe.
— ALAN WATTS

To demand "sense" is the hallmark of nonsense. Nature does not make sense. Nothing makes sense.
— AYN RAND

Men argue, nature acts.   — VOLTAIRE

The universe is not hostile, nor yet is it friendly. It is simply indifferent.   — JOHN H. HOLMES

The mastery of nature is vainly believed to be an adequate substitute for self-mastery.
— REINHOLD NIEBUHR

Drive Nature from your door with a pitchfork, and she will return again and again.   — HORACE

Nature is an infinite sphere of which the center is everywhere, and the circumference nowhere.   — PASCAL

Even the most rational man has need of nature again from time to time.   — NIETZSCHE

NEUROSIS

When we remember that we are all mad, the mysteries disappear and life stands explained.   — MARK TWAIN

Everything great in the world comes from neurotics. They alone have founded our religions, and composed our masterpieces. Never will the world know all it owes to them, nor all they have suffered to enrich us.

— PROUST

One is healthy when one can laugh at the earnestness and zeal with which one has been hypnotized by any single detail of one's life.   — NIETZSCHE

NONEXISTENCE and NON-BEING

Nothing is more important than the existence of what does not exist.   — JOHN HAWKES

Pure Being and pure non-being are the same thing.
— HEGEL

Being is no more than not-Being.   — HERACLITUS

The true, unique and perpetual object of thought is the nonexistent!   — PAUL VALERY

The absence of something is not merely that.
— PROUST

I tend a garden whose blossom never existed.
— PABLO NERUDA

NOTHING

There is nothing, and it is this nothing which does everything.   — JEAN COCTEAU

Every something is an echo of nothing. — JOHN CAGE

Every moment is nothing without end. — OCTAVIO PAZ

It was a nothing that he knew too well. It was all a nothing and a man was nothing too. It was only that and light was all it needed and a certain cleanness and order. Some lived in it and never felt it but he knew it all was nada y pues nada y nada y pues nada. Our nada who art in nada, nada be thy name thy kingdom nada thy will be nada in nada as it is in nada. Give us this nada our daily nada and nada us our nada as we nada our nadas and nada us not into nada but deliver us from nada; pues nada. Hail nothing full of nothing, nothing is with thee. — HEMINGWAY

I came from nothing—I shall be nothing.
— GREEK PROVERB

Nothing exists. — ZENO

Nothing is often a good thing to do and always a good thing to say. — WILL DURANT

There is not enough nothing in it. — JOHN CAGE

Even a good thing isn't as good as nothing.
— ZEN BUDDHIST SAYING

The something which I am...is precisely a nothing.
— KIERKEGAARD

A variety of nothing is superior to a monotony of something. — JEAN PAUL RICHTER

How beautiful it is to do nothing, and then rest afterward. — SPANISH PROVERB

It takes a long time to understand nothing.
— EDWARD DAHLBERG

Every man has a deep instinct that is neither for destruction nor creation—simply the longing to resemble nothing. — CAMUS

I have never waited for anything the way I've waited for today, when nothing will happen.
— MARGUERITE DURAS

I hear nothings, I speak nothings, I take interest in nothing, and from nothing to nothing I travel gently down the dull way which leads to becoming nothing.
— MADAME du DEFFAND

Perhaps this is much ado about nothing.
— SHAKESPEARE

This very real world of ours, with all its suns and galaxies, is—nothing. — SCHOPENHAUER

Ex nihilo omne ens qua ens fit: every being, so far as it is a being, is made out of nothing. — HEIDEGGER

Nothing is more real than nothing.
— SAMUEL BECKETT

Nothing is anything. — RANIER MARIA RILKE

Nothing more than nothing can be said.— JOHN CAGE

The NOTHINGNESS

Among the great things which are to be found among us, the Being of Nothingness is the greatest.
— LEONARDO da VINCI

What I sought was the rapture of vertigo...the relapse...to nothingness.
— SAMUEL BECKETT

Everything depends on this: a fathomless sinking into a fathomless nothingness.
— JOHANNES TAULER

God made everything out of nothing, but the nothingness shows through.
— PAUL VALERY

Men fear silence as they fear solitude, because both give them a glimpse of the terror of life's nothingness.
— ANDRE MAUROIS

Utterances about the Nothing must always remain unusual. It cannot be made common.
— HEIDEGGER

Nothingness carries being in its heart.
— SARTRE

What can be seductive about the eternal nothing is that the finest day is indifferently this one or any other like it.
— RENE CHAR

At any streetcorner the feeling of absurdity can strike any man in the face.
— CAMUS

Only because of...the revelation of Nothing, does the "why?" spring to our lips.
— HEIDEGGER

Man would sooner have the void for his purpose than be
void of purpose. — NIETZSCHE

The void is waiting for a vocabulary.
— EDMOND JABES

The hypothesis of absolute void contains nothing at all
which terrifies me. I am ready to fling myself into the
great black hole with perfect calm.
— GUSTAVE FLAUBERT

... what seemed abyss becomes the space of freedom:
the seeming Nothingness turns into that from which true
Being speaks to us. — KARL JASPERS

Man is perishable. That may be; but let us perish resist-
ing, and if it is nothingness that awaits us, let us so act
that it shall be an unjust fate.
— MIGUEL de UNAMUNO

In an utter emptiness anything can take place.
— JOHN CAGE

OBJECTS

To restore silence is the role of objects.
— SAMUEL BECKETT

Everything that becomes an object to me approaches
me...from the dark background of Being.
— HEIDEGGER

The noblest function of an object is to be contemplated.
— MIGUEL de UNAMUNO

Things have their laws as well as men, and things refuse to be trifled with. — EMERSON

The goal of all inanimate objects is to resist man and finally to defeat him. — RUSSELL BAKER

ONE

A man's life's no more than to say "One."
— SHAKESPEARE

One is more than a multitude. — BEN JONSON

And everything comes to One, / As we dance on, dance on, dance on. — ROETHKE

All wisdom comes out of one center, and the number of wisdom is one. — PARACELSUS

PAIN

There are no true beginnings but in pain.
— LESLIE WOOLF HEDLEY

The greatest evil is physical pain.
— ST. AUGUSTINE of HIPPO

One hour of pain is a better teacher than all the philosophers put together. — PASCAL

In the country of pain we are each alone.
— MAY SARTON

PARADOX

Having never been definitively modeled, man is the harborer of his opposite.   — RENE CHAR

He who confronts the paradoxical exposes himself to reality.   — FRIEDRICH DURRENMATT

Life is a paradox. Every truth has its counterpart which contradicts it; and every philosopher supplies the logic for his undoing.   — ELBERT HUBBARD

Only the paradox comes anywhere near to comprehending the fullness of life.   — CARL JUNG

Truth is always paradoxical.   — THOREAU

The paradox is the source of the thinker's passion, and the thinker without a paradox is like a lover without feeling; a paltry mediocrity.   — KIERKEGAARD

The greatest music cannot be heard. / The greatest form has no shape.   — TAO TE CHING

One of the ordinary weaknesses of the human intellect is to seek to reconcile contrary principles, and to purchase peace at the expense of logic.
                — ALEXIS de TOCQUEVILLE

PASSION

When the passions become masters, they are vices.
                — PASCAL

If we resist our passions, it is due more to their weakness than to our own strength.
— FRANCOIS de la ROCHEFOUCAULD

The PAST

One cannot be and have been.   — FRENCH PROVERB

Life could not continue without throwing the past into the past, liberating the present from its burden.
— PAUL TILLICH

Respect the past in the full measure of it desserts, but do not make the mistake of confusing it with the present nor seek in it the ideals of the future.
— JOSE INGENIEROS

In reality, the past changes as rapidly as the present.
— LUDWIG GOLDSCHEIDER

Never turn back and never believe that an hour is better because it is dead.   — BERYL MARKHAM

We need not destroy the past: it is gone; at any moment it might reappear and seem to be and be the present.
— JOHN CAGE

Through loyalty to the past, our mind refuses to realize that tomorrow's joy is possible only if today's makes way for it; that each wave owes the beauty of its line only to the withdrawal of the preceding one.   — ANDRE GIDE

The past is not the past, but it is here, now, / and in the silence of the present, it fills / into another moment which vanishes. — OCTAVIO PAZ

The past is a foreign country; they do things differently there. — LESLEY P. HARTLEY

I am not my past. — SARTRE

What's past is prologue. — SHAKESPEARE

The past is no more than a belief. — PAUL VALERY

PERCEPTION

If the doors of perception were cleansed everything would appear to man as it is, infinite.
— WILLIAM BLAKE

All our knowledge has its origins in our perception.
— LEONARDO da VINCI

A work is never perceived. It is received.
— JEAN COCTEAU

The day is coming when a single carrot, freshly observed, will set off a revolution. — CEZANNE

To see is to forget the name of the thing one sees.
— PAUL VALERY

The moon is a different thing to each one of us.
— FRANK BORMAN

What I perceive is also what I know.   — SARTRE

For me the familiar and unfamiliar lie everywhere together, like two enormous faces back to back. I am always seeing the man in the child, the child in the grown man. Winter is my time of flowers, I am a resigned but spirited voyager.   — JOHN HAWKES

PHILOSOPHY

I care for a philosopher only to the extent that he is able to serve as an example.   — NIETZSCHE

The name is misleading insofar as it seems to restrict. Philosophy can never wish to be less than primordial, eternal philosophy itself.   — KARL JASPERS

Example moves the world more than doctrine.
                    — HENRY MILLER

The true philosopher, who is not one chiefly by profession, must be prepared to tread the wine press alone.
                    — SANTAYANA

Only as an individual can man become a philosopher.
                    — KARL JASPERS

Philosophy triumphs easily over past and future evils; but present evils triumph over it.
                    — FRANCOIS de la ROCHEFOUCAULD

Judging whether life is or is not worth living amounts to answering the fundamental question of philosophy. All the rest—whether or not the world has three dimensions, whether the mind has nine or twelve categories—comes afterwards. These are games; one must first answer.
— CAMUS

He's a philosopher in his own way: he thinks only of himself, the rest of the universe counting for nothing with him.
— DENIS DIDEROT

A blind man in a dark room—looking for a black hat which isn't there.
— LORD BOWEN

Philosophy with its way of thinking is in the same order only with poetry.
— HEIDEGGER

In philosophy an individual is becoming himself.
— BERNARD LONERGAN

Philosophy can pay attention to but cannot nourish us.
— KIERKEGAARD

Be a philosopher but, amidst all your philosophy, be still a man.
— DAVID HUME

True philosophy scoffs at philosophy.
— PASCAL

Philosophy is not a body of doctrine but an activity.
— LUDWIG WITTGENSTEIN

No condition of life could be so well adapted for the practice of philosophy as this in which chance finds you today!
— MARCUS AURELIUS

PLACES and TRAVEL

Wherever we are content, that is our country.
— MARCUS PACUVIUS

Paradise is wherever I am. — VOLTAIRE

I travel not to go anywhere, but to go...the great affair is to move. — ROBERT LOUIS STEVENSON

The journey is the reward. — EMERSON

Make voyages! Attempt them! There's nothing else.
— TENNESSEE WILLIAMS

I am always moving. I am forever transporting myself somewhere else. I am never exactly where I am.
— JOHN HAWKES

Every perfect traveler always creates the country where he travels. — NIKOS KAZANTZAKIS

There is no country for those who despair. — CAMUS

Nothing will have taken place but the place.
— MALLARME

I used to wonder / About here and there— / I think the distance / Is nowhere. — LANGSTON HUGHES

A good traveler is one who does not know where he is going to, and a perfect traveler does not know where he came from. — LIN YUTANG

I have traveled so much because travel has enabled me to arrive at unknown places within my clouded self.
— LAURENS VAN DER POST

PLEASURE

Enjoy pleasures, but let them be your own, and then you will taste them.   — LORD CHESTERFIELD

People have many different kinds of pleasure. The real one is the one for which they will forsake all others.
— PROUST

Pleasure is the object, the duty, and the goal of all rational creatures.   — VOLTAIRE

No man is a hypocrite in his pleasures.   — CAMUS

Draw your pleasure—paint your pleasure—express your pleasure strongly.   — PIERRE BONNARD

To be for one day entirely at leisure is to be for one day an immortal.   — CHINESE PROVERB

POETRY and POETS

Poetry makes nothing happen: it survives in the valley of its saying.   — W. H. AUDEN

I have nothing to say and I am saying it and that is poetry.   — JOHN CAGE

A poem should not mean / But be.

— ARCHIBALD MACLEISH

There is no advice to give young poets.

— PABLO NERUDA

A poem, a sentence, causes us to see ourselves. I be, and see my being, at the same time.   — EMERSON

Poetry is a religion with no hope.   — JEAN COCTEAU

I dream of a poetry which says nothing. — LaFORGUE

Poetry will rob me of my death.   — RENE CHAR

Poetry is the opening and closing of a door, leaving those who look through to guess what is seen during a moment.   — CARL SANDBURG

Poetry is an ethic.   — JEAN COCTEAU

It is difficult / to get the news from poems / yet men die miserably every day / for lack / of what is found there.

— WILLIAM CARLOS WILLIAMS

And here I am, the / center of all beauty! / writing these poems! / imagine!   — FRANK O'HARA

A good poem is a contribution to reality.

— DYLAN THOMAS

So poetry is something more philosophical and more worthy of serious attention than history.— ARISTOTLE

The ideal is to suggest. — MALLARME

POSSIBILITY and the POSSIBLE

Higher than actuality stands possibility. — HEIDEGGER

All knowledge about reality is possibility.
— KIERKEGAARD

O my soul, do not aspire to immortal life, but exhaust the limits of the possible. — PINDAR

The world is mine because it is haunted by possibilities.
— SARTRE

Knowledge of what is possible is the beginning of happiness. — SANTAYANA

To return what exists to pure possibility; to reduce what is seen to pure visibility; that is the deep, the hidden work.
— PAUL VALERY

Even a thought, even a possibility, can shatter us and transform us. — NIETZSCHE

If God didn't exist, everything would be possible.
— DOSTOEVSKY

We turn toward God only to obtain the impossible. As for the possible, men suffice. — LEO CHESTOV

I am my possibilities. — GABRIEL MARCEL

To my mind, the possible and the future are one.
— ANDRE GIDE

PRECEDENT

If you're strong enough, there *are* no precedents.
— F. SCOTT FITZGERALD

There are no precedents: You are the only You that ever was.
— CHRISTOPHER MORLEY

THE PRESENT

Nothing was, nothing will be, everything has reality and presence.
— HERMANN HESSE

Be intent upon the perfection of the present day.
— WILLIAM LAW

Real generosity toward the future lies in giving all to the present.
— CAMUS

Life is only an infinite succession of nows.
— JOHN KILLINGER

The word "now" is like a bomb through the window, and it ticks.
— ARTHUR MILLER

Now and always.
— ITALIAN EXPRESSION

The present is the only thing with no end.
— ERWIN SCHRODINGER

My time is today. — GEORGE GERSHWIN

Existence must be asserted in the present if one does not want all life to be defined as an escape toward nothingness. — SIMONE de BEAUVOIR

I have realized that the past and the future are real illusions, that they exist only in the present, which is what there is and all that there is. — ALAN WATTS

No yesterdays are ever wasted for those who give themselves to today. — BRENDAN FRANCIS

The present moment is a powerful goddess.
— GOETHE

No one suspects the days to be gods. — EMERSON

It is difficult to conceive of permanence without the present. — JUAN RAMON JIMENEZ

With the Past, as past, I have nothing to do; nor with the Future as future. I live now, and will verify all past history in my own moments. — EMERSON

The present moment alone is man's.
— SAMUEL JOHNSON

I am in the present. I cannot know what tomorrow will bring forth. I can know only what the truth is for me today. That is what I am called upon to serve, and I serve it in all lucidity. — IGOR STRAVINSKY

Presence is not what is evanescent and passes but what confronts us, waiting and enduring. — MARTIN BUBER

Nothing is worth more than this day.   — GOETHE

PRIDE

It is as proper to have pride in oneself as it is ridiculous to show it to others.
— FRANCOIS de la ROCHEFOUCAULD

PRINCIPLE

Principle never forgives and its logic is to kill.
— JACQUES BARZUN

Rise above principle and do what's right.
— WALTER HELLER

PROGRESS

Man's "progress" is but a gradual discovery that his questions have no meaning.   — SAINT-EXUPERY

The only real progress lies in learning to be wrong all alone.   — CAMUS

All progress means war with Society.
— BERNARD SHAW

I do not believe in the indefinite progress of Societies. I believe in man's progress over himself. — BALZAC

I am still progressing. — RENOIR (last words)

QUOTATIONS

I often quote myself. It adds spice to my conversation.
— BERNARD SHAW

I quote others to better express myself. — MONTAIGNE

REALITY

Be it life or death, we crave only reality. — THOREAU

They thought I was a surrealist, but I wasn't. I never painted dreams. I painted my own reality.
— FRIDA KAHLO

Since human reality is act, it can be conceived only as being at its core a rupture with the given. — SARTRE

My care is for myself; / Myself am whole and sole reality. — ROBERT BROWNING

There is no reality except the one contained within us. That is why so many people live such an unreal life. They take images outside them for reality and never allow the world within to assert itself. — HERMANN HESSE

Man is a reality and humanity an abstraction.

— KOESTLER

In the world *man* alone is the reality which is accessible to me.

— KARL JASPERS

Reality is possible only at the price of solitude.

— RANIER MARIA RILKE

Between reality and its report, there is your life which magnifies reality.

— RENE CHAR

Reality is where we are from moment to moment.

— ROBERT LINSSEN

Reality is a staircase going neither up nor down, we don't move, today is today, always is today.

— JUAN RAMON JIMENEZ

REASON

To an absurd mind reason is useless and there is nothing beyond reason.

— CAMUS

Reason has no assured stability: it is constantly on the move.

— KARL JASPERS

Reason is Thought determining itself in absolute freedom.

— HEGEL

Reason does not exist by nature but only by decision.

— KARL JASPERS

Reason is also choice.   — JOHN MILTON

Reason, itself the origin of order, attends even the powers which destroy order.   — KARL JASPERS

Our reason has driven all away. Alone at last, we end up by ruling over a desert.   — CAMUS

Logic is doubtless unshakable, but it cannot withstand a man who wants to go on living.   — KAFKA

Reason is only reason, and it can only satisfy the reasoning ability of man, whereas volition is a manifestation of the whole of life.   — DOSTOEVSKY

RELATIONSHIPS (the Self and Others)

Whoever says You does not have something; he has nothing. But he stands in relation.   — MARTIN BUBER

To be conscious of another is to be conscious of what one is not.   — SARTRE

The bonds that unite another person to ourself exist only in our mind.   — PROUST

We never touch but at points.   — EMERSON

A good marriage is one in which each appoints the other guardian of his solitude.   — RANIER MARIA RILKE

It is not the failed relationships which influence our life— they influence our death.   — ANAIS NIN

My closest relation is myself.   — TERENCE

Do not do unto others as you would they should do unto you. Their tastes may not be the same.
                                    — BERNARD SHAW

RELIGION, FAITH, and GOD

I wonder if we could contrive...some magnificent myth that would in itself carry conviction to our whole community.   — PLATO

That which has been believed by everyone, always and everywhere, has every chance of being false.
                                    — PAUL VALERY

I am the first one in the whole history of mankind who would not invent God.   — DOSTOEVSKY

Convictions are more dangerous foes of the truth than lies.   — NIETZSCHE

By the year 2000 we will, I hope, raise our children to believe in human potential, not God.
                                    — GLORIA STEINEM

One's religion is whatever he's most interested in.
                                    — J. M. BARRIE

For everything that lives is holy, life delights in life.
                                    — WILLIAM BLAKE

The courage not to believe in anything.
— IVAN TURGENEV

A faith that does not perpetually expose itself to the possibility of unfaith is no faith but merely a convenience.
— HEIDEGGER

"Faith" means not *wanting* to know what is true.
— NIETZSCHE

Faith is believing what you know ain't so.
— MARK TWAIN

I myself tend to think of catching trains more than Christianity.
— JOHN CAGE

One real world is enough.
— SANTAYANA

Our Father which art in heaven / Stay there / And we will stay on earth / which sometimes is so pretty.
— JACQUES PREVERT

I neglect God and his angels for the noise of a fly, for the rattling of a coach, for the whining of a door.
— JOHN DONNE

There is a very good saying that if triangles had invented a god, they would have made him three-sided.
— BARON de MONTESQUIEU

Almost two thousand years, and no new god!
— NIETZSCHE

Surrounded by monsters and gods, we know no calm.
— PROUST

Beware the man whose god is in the skies.
— BERNARD SHAW

Silence is God. Absence is God. God is the loneliness of man.
— SARTRE

God's only excuse is that he does not exist.
— STENDAHL

If God does not exist, then I am God. — DOSTOEVSKY

God, to me, it seems / is a verb.
— R. BUCKMINSTER FULLER

God is dead.
— NIETZSCHE

I've never felt sorry about losing God, for He had robbed me of the earth.
— SIMONE de BEAUVOIR

I have never wished that there was a god to call on—I have often wished there was a God to thank.
— F. SCOTT FITZGERALD

Refine your reasoning, expel your prejudices, and you will no longer need your God.
— DOSTOEVSKY

I feel no need for any other faith than my faith in human beings.
— PEARL S. BUCK

We have lost religion but we have found humanism.
— SARTRE

Nontheism is conversely a belief in Man.

— THOMAS E. KELLY

REPETITION

Repetition is the same movement as memory, but going the other way.
— KIERKEGAARD

Repetition is the only form of permanence that nature can achieve.
— SANTAYANA

Believing in repeating is one way of being.
— GERTRUDE STEIN

The thousand times he had proved it meant nothing. Now he was proving it again. Each time was a new time and he never thought about the past when he was doing it.
— HEMINGWAY

Act is virgin. Even repeated.
— RENE CHAR

RESPONSIBILITY

The first effect of existentialism is that it puts every man in possession of himself as he is, and places the entire responsibility for his existence squarely upon his own shoulders.
— SARTRE

Life has no meaning except in terms of responsibility.
— REINHOLD NEIBUHR

To be a man is, precisely, to be responsible.
— SAINT-EXUPERY

Every damn thing is your own fault if you're any good.
— HEMINGWAY

In dreams begin responsibility.
— WILLIAM BUTLER YEATS

To become free and responsible. For this alone was man created.
— DAG HAMMARSKJOLD

REVENGE

To refrain from imitation is the best revenge.
— MARCUS AURELIUS

RISK and DANGER

Believe me! The secret to realizing the greatest fruitfulness and the greatest enjoyment is: to *live dangerously*.
— NIETZSCHE

I have always felt I lived on the high seas, threatened, at the heart of a royal happiness.
— CAMUS

During the first part of a man's life, the danger is not to take the risk.
— KIERKEGAARD

Draw your chair up close to the edge of the precipice and I'll tell you a story.
— F. SCOTT FITZGERALD

Better to live one day as a lion than a hundred years as a sheep.
— HEMINGWAY

The danger lies in the subtle instant that precedes the leap.   — CAMUS

The SELF

Wherever we go, whatever we do, self is the sole subject we study and learn.   — EMERSON

There is only one great adventure and that is inward towards the self.   — HENRY MILLER

When you come right down to it all you have is yourself. The sun is a thousand rays in your belly. All the rest is nothing.   — PICASSO

When you turn the corner / And run into *yourself* / Then you know that you have turned / All the corners that are left.   — LANGSTON HUGHES

I am playing with my Self, I am playing with the world's soul, I am the dialogue between my Self and *el espiritu del mundo*. I change myself, I change the world.   — GLORIA ANZALDUA

I celebrate myself, and sing myself. — WALT WHITMAN

SELF-ASSERTION

What saves a man is to take a step. Then another step. It is always the same step, but you have to take it.   — SAINT-EXUPERY

To know oneself, one should assert oneself. — CAMUS

First say to yourself what you would be; and then do what you have to do. — EPICTETUS

SELF-CONFIDENCE

As is our confidence, so is our capacity.
— WILLIAM HAZLITT

They do all because they think they can. — VIRGIL

There's one blessing only, the source and cornerstone of beatitude—confidence in the self. — SENECA

Trust me, but look to thyself. — IRISH PROVERB

Trust yourself, then you will know how to live.
— GOETHE

SELF-CONTROL

Not being able to govern events, I govern myself, and apply myself to them, if they will not apply themselves to me. — MONTAIGNE

Man who man would be, must rule the empire of himself. — PERCY BYSSHE SHELLEY

I am, / indeed, / a king, because I know how / to rule myself. — PIETRO ARETINO

I am master of myself as of the universe.

— PIERRE CORNEILLE

Conquer yourself rather than the world. — DESCARTES

If you are distressed by anything external, the pain is not due to the thing itself, but to your own estimation of it; and this you have the power to revoke at any moment.

— MARCUS AURELIUS

To be in hell is to drift; to be in heaven is to steer.

— BERNARD SHAW

The man who masters himself is delivered from the force that binds all creatures.   — GOETHE

A man who is master of himself can end a sorrow as easily as he can invent a pleasure.   — OSCAR WILDE

Lord of himself, that heritage of woe. — LORD BYRON

I live in my own place / have never copied nobody even half, / and at any master who lacks the grace / to laugh at himself—I laugh.

— Inscription over NIETZSCHE's door

SELF-DECEPTION

We are never deceived; we deceive ourselves.

— GOETHE

Nature never deceives us; it is we who deceive ourselves.

— ROUSSEAU

SELF-DETERMINATION

Every man is the son of his own works. — CERVANTES

Man's main task in life is to give birth to himself.
— ERICH FROMM

Where I was born and where and how I have lived is unimportant. It is what I have done with where I have been that should be of interest. — GEORGIA O'KEEFE

Every man is his own absolute lawgiver and dispenser of glory or gloom to himself, the maker of his life, his reward, his punishment. — UNKNOWN

I tell you that each of us, privately, is pretty well limited to what he says to himself, and what he says to himself is limited to what he is capable of saying. — PAUL VALERY

Let each man now establish his worth. — PASCAL

People often say that this or that person has not yet found himself. But the self is not something that one finds. It is something one creates. — THOMAS SZASZ

SELF-INJURY

The fearful Unbelief is unbelief in yourself.
— THOMAS CARLYLE

Our greatest foes, and whom we must chiefly combat, are within. — CERVANTES

I, who have never willfully pained another, have no business to pain myself. — MARCUS AURELIUS

It is a painful thing / To look at your own trouble and know / That you yourself and no one else has made it.
— SOPHOCLES

I am always with myself, and it is I who am my tormentor. — TOLSTOY

SELF-INTEREST

It is easy to live for others; everybody does. I call on you to live for yourselves. — EMERSON

I am a man who does not exist for others. — AYN RAND

Men are not against you; they are simply for themselves.
— GENE FOWLER

Let me listen to me and not to them.
— GERTRUDE STEIN

Lend yourself to others, but give yourself to yourself.
— MONTAIGNE

SELF-KNOWLEDGE

Gnothi seauton. (Know thyself.)
— Inscription at the Temple of Apollo at Delphi

Wherever we look, we see ourselves all too clearly.
— GEORG CHRISTOPH LICHTENBERG

Today I have got myself out of all my perplexities; or rather, I have got the perplexities out of myself—for they were not without, but within; they lay in my own outlook.
— MARCUS AURELIUS

I have interrogated you—he said. And for the duration of my questioning, we were, both of us...only the vertigo of an infinite question put to ourselves.
— EDMOND JABES

We gain a great deal in life if we learn how to remain perfectly natural and sincere towards ourselves, and only to love what we truly love, and not—out of pride or false emulation—to prolong passions already dead.
— CHARLES AUGUSTIN SAINT-BEUVE

Nobody knows what's in him until he tries to pull it out. If there's nothing, or very little, the shock can kill a man.
— HEMINGWAY

Know thyself? If I knew myself, I'd run away.
— GOETHE

Were man to begin with the study of himself, he would see how incapable he is of proceeding further.
— PASCAL

"I know myself," he cried, "but that is all!"
— F. SCOTT FITZGERALD

SELF-LOVE

I conceived at least one great love in my life, of which I was always the object.   — CAMUS

Self-love, my liege, is not so vile a sin as self-neglecting.
                                      — SHAKESPEARE

One must learn to love oneself...with a wholesome and healthy love, so that one can bear to be with oneself and need not roam.   — NIETZSCHE

Self-love seems so often unrequited.
                              — ANTHONY POWELL

The good man ought to be a lover of self, since he will then act nobly, and so benefit himself and aid his fellows.   — ARISTOTLE

Anyone who loves himself so intently transforms everything that emanates from him into wealth.
                           — NATHALIE SARRAUTE

SELF-RESPECT

We've been taught to respect our fears, but we must learn to respect ourselves and our needs. — AUDRE LOURDE

Respect yourself if you would have others respect you.
                              — BALTASAR GRACIAN

The noble soul has reverence for itself. — NIETZSCHE

SELF-SUFFICIENCY

Happiness belongs to the self-sufficient. — ARISTOTLE

I'll walk where my own nature would be leading— / It vexes me to choose another guide. — EMILY BRONTE

I believe that the prime indication of a well-ordered mind is a man's ability to remain in one place and to linger in his own company. — SENECA

A man can stand a lot as long as he can stand himself. He can live without hope, without friends, without books, even without music, as long as he can listen to his own thoughts. — ALEX MUNTHE

I swear by my life and the love of it that I will never live for the sake of another man, nor ask another man to live for mine. — AYN RAND (Motto of Atlantis)

Be faithful to that which exists nowhere but in yourself— and thus make yourself indispensable.
— ANDRE GIDE

Be thine own palace, or the world's thy jail.
— JOHN DONNE

The only defences that are good, certain, and lasting, are those that depend on yourself alone and on your own ability. — NICCOLO MACHIAVELLI

For an impenetrable shield, stand inside yourself.
— THOREAU

Self-sufficiency is the greatest of all wealth.
— EPICURUS

The greatest fruit of self-sufficiency is freedom.
— EPICURUS

The proverb warns that, "You should not bite the hand that feeds you." But maybe you should, if it prevents you from feeding yourself. — THOMAS SZASZ

Let me hack at my own vines. — HORACE

Cast off everything that is not yourself. — PERSIUS

Our remedies oft in ourselves lie, / which we ascribe to heaven. — SHAKESPEARE

The SENSES

All credibility, all good conscience, all evidence of truth come only from the senses. — NIETZSCHE

The five senses within whose pentagon each man is alone. — JOHN BERGER

Feelings and images multiply a philosophy by ten.
— CAMUS

The great art of life is sensation, to feel that we exist, even in pain. — LORD BYRON

The wise reject what they think, not what they see.
— HUANG PO

We are astonished at thought, but sensation is equally wonderful. — VOLTAIRE

To see is to forget the name of the thing one sees.
— PAUL VALERY

To see one must go beyond the imagination and for that one must stand absolutely still as though at the center of a leap. — JOHN CAGE

A sound accomplishes nothing: without it life would not last out the instant. — JOHN CAGE

A morning-glory at my window satisfies me more than the metaphysics of my books. — WALT WHITMAN

Perhaps to our senses things offer only their rejections. Perfume is what the flowers throw away.
— PAUL VALERY

SILENCE

Silence is the element in which great things fashion themselves. — THOMAS CARLYLE

People have the acoustic illusion that where nothing is heard there is nothing. — NIETZSCHE

Not one sound fears the silence that extinguishes it.
— JOHN CAGE

An absolute silence leads to sadness: it is the image of death. — ROUSSEAU

It takes a man to make a room silent.   — THOREAU

May my silences become more accurate.   — ROETHKE

Silence is the essential condition of happiness.
                                — HEINRICH HEINE

Silence is health.   — Motto on the obelisk in the
                          Avienda 9 de Julio, Buenos Aires

Silence was his only sensation.   — AYN RAND

Her hearing was keener than his, and she heard silences
he was unaware of.   — D.M. THOMAS

We count on blood resembling blood in our thirst for
silence. / Solitude under the skin.   — EDMOND JABES

SIMPLICITY

Everything should be made as simple as possible, but
not simpler.   — ALBERT EINSTEIN

SIN

If there is a sin against this life, it consists perhaps not so
much in despairing of life as in hoping for another, and
in eluding the implacable grandeur of this life.
                                — CAMUS

The sin of being another being.
                                — SIMONE de BEAUVOIR

The only sin is mediocrity.   — MARTHA GRAHAM

Sin is whatever obscures the soul.   — ANDRE GIDE

As long as man has existed, man has enjoyed himself
too little: that alone, my brothers, is our original sin!
                                        — NIETZSCHE

The greatest crimes are caused by surfeit, not by want.
                                        — ARISTOTLE

We are sinful not merely because we have eaten of the
Tree of Knowledge, but also because we have not yet
eaten of the Tree of Life.   — KAFKA

SOCIETY

The degree of a nation's civilization is marked by its dis-
regard for the necessities of existence.
                              — W. SOMERSET MAUGHAM

Civilization only produces a greater variety of sensations
in man—and absolutely nothing more.
                                        — DOSTOEVSKY

"Mankind" does not advance, it does not even exist.
                                        — NIETZSCHE

Other people are quite dreadful. The only possible society is one's self.   — OSCAR WILDE

Society is no comfort / To one not sociable.
                                        — SHAKESPEARE

Hell is other people. — SARTRE

SOLITUDE

Solitude is a product that is made everywhere.
— PAUL VALERY

The happiest of all lives is a busy solitude. — VOLTAIRE

I have never found the companion that was so companionable as solitude. — THOREAU

Nothing will change the fact that I cannot produce the least thing without absolute solitude. — GOETHE

To dare to live alone is the rarest courage; since there are many who had rather meet their bitterest enemy in the field, than their own hearts in their closet.
— CHARLES CALEB COLTON

Inside myself there is a place where I live all alone and that's where you renew your springs that never dry up.
— PEARL S. BUCK

Night, when words fade and things come alive, when the destructive analysis of the day is done, and all that is truly important becomes whole and sound again. When man reassembles his fragmentary self and grows with the calm of a tree. — SAINT-EXUPERY

Like a lonely fir tree...looking toward something higher, I stand there, throwing no shadow. — KIERKEGAARD

Solitary trees, if they grow at all, grow strong.
— WINSTON CHURCHILL

If you are alone, you will be your own man.
— LEONARDO da VINCI

To be alone is the fate of all great minds—a fate deplorable at times, but still always chosen as the less grievous of two evils.
— SCHOPENHAUER

It is bitter to be alone...bitter, bitter, bitter, bitter. There is no end to it, it is fathomless, and it is the lot of every man on earth, but especially mine...especially mine.
— HENRY MILLER

We are dancing in the hollow of nothingness. We are of one flesh, but separated like stars.
— HENRY MILLER

Life is for each man a solitary cell whose walls are mirrors.
— EUGENE O'NEILL

Anything we fully do is an alone journey.
— NATALIE GOLDBERG

I admit my solitude—there is no other way.
— JEAN COCTEAU

Solitude, as death proves, is our natural state.
— HEMINGWAY

You find in solitude only what you take to it.
— JUAN RAMON JIMENEZ

This great pain, the inability to be alone.
— LaBRUYERE

I was never less alone than when I was by myself.
— EDWARD GIBBON

Whosoever is delighted in solitude is either a beast or a god.
— FRANCIS BACON

I am solitude become man.
— NIETZSCHE

SORROW and DESPAIR

You may not know it, but at the far end of despair, there is a white clearing where one is almost happy.
— JEAN ANOUILH

Life begins on the other side of despair.
— SARTRE

Despair lames most people, but it wakes others fully up.
— WILLIAM JAMES

Between grief and nothing I will take grief.
— WILLIAM FAULKNER

But behind sorrow there is only sorrow. Pain, unlike pleasure, wears no mask.
— OSCAR WILDE

Grief can't be shared. Everyone carries it alone, his own burden, his own way. — ANNE MORROW LINDBERGH

A calm despair...is the essence of wisdom.
— ALFRED de VIGNY

Some men are above grief and some men are below it.

— EMERSON

No one could be more unhappy than a man who has never known affliction. — DEMETRIUS of PHALERUM

So then choose despair, for even despair has a choice.

— KIERKEGAARD

It is a misery to know one's misery, but to recognize it is to be great.

— PASCAL

The keenest sorrow is to recognize ourselves as the sole cause of all our adversities.

— SOPHOCLES

What man is there that does not laboriously, though all unconsciously, himself fashion the sorrow that is to be the pivot of his life.

— MAURICE MAETERLINCK

There are times when sorrow seems to be the only truth.

— OSCAR WILDE

Grief is the agony of an instant; the indulgence of grief the blunder of a life.

— BENJAMIN DISRAELI

Grief teaches the steadiest minds to waver.

— HERACLITUS

Sadness is almost never anything but a form of fatigue.

— ANDRE GIDE

Not to be one's own self is despair.

— KIERKEGAARD

It is better to learn early of the inevitable depths, for then sorrow and death take their proper place in life, and one is not afraid. — PEARL S. BUCK

Let us remember that sorrow alone is the creator of great things. — ERNEST RENAN

My only hope lies in my despair. — RACINE

Don't despair—not even over the fact that you don't despair. — KAFKA

Despair of nothing. — LATIN PROVERB

Out of my great woe / I make my little song.
— HEINRICH HEINE

SPEECH

No one would talk so much in society, if he only knew how often he misunderstands others. — GOETHE

True eloquence consists in saying all that should be said, and that only. — FRANCOIS de la ROCHEFOUCAULD

Drawing on my fine command of language, I said nothing. — ROBERT BENCHLEY

You lose it if you talk about it. — HEMINGWAY

Speech is of time, silence is of eternity.
— THOMAS CARLYLE

His very silence speaks volumes.　— LATIN PROVERB

In being said—or not said—the void is voided.
　　　　　　　　　　　　　　　— EDMOND JABES

What can be said at all can be said clearly.
　　　　　　　　　　　— LUDWIG WITTGENSTEIN

Do not *say* things. What you *are* stands over you the while, and thunders so that I cannot hear what you say to the contrary.　　　　　　　　— EMERSON

Never to talk of oneself is a form of hypocrisy.
　　　　　　　　　　　　　　　— NIETZSCHE

What I am I am, and say not. Being is the great explainer.
　　　　　　　　　　　　　　　— THOREAU

STRENGTH

The strongest man in the world is he who stands most alone.　　　　　　　　　— HENRIK IBSEN

That which does not kill me makes me stronger.
　　　　　　　　　　　　　　　— NIETZSCHE

In the depth of winter, I finally learned that within me there lay an invincible summer.　　　— CAMUS

Deep in their roots, / All flowers keep the light.
　　　　　　　　　　　　　　　— ROETHKE

SUCCESS

There is only one success—to be able to spend your own life in your own way.   — CHRISTOPHER MORLEY

If one advances confidently in the direction of his dreams, and endeavors to live the life which he has imagined, he will meet with a success unexpected in common hours.   — THOREAU

Nobody knows what I am trying to do but I do and I know when I succeed.   — GERTRUDE STEIN

SUFFERING

Profound suffering makes noble; it separates.   — NIETZSCHE

I leave Sisyphus at the foot of the mountain! One always finds one's burden again.   — CAMUS

Suffering is the sole origin of consciousness.   — DOSTOEVSKY

Although the world is full of suffering, it is also full of the overcoming of it.   — HELEN KELLER

We are healed of a suffering only by experiencing it to the full.   — PROUST

What really raises one's indignation against suffering is not suffering intrinsically, but the senselessness of suffering.   — NIETZSCHE

Man is sometimes extraordinarily, passionately in love with suffering. — DOSTOEVSKY

I am the man, I suffered, I was there.
— WALT WHITMAN

SUICIDE

There is but one truly serious philosophical problem, and that is suicide. — CAMUS

The thought of suicide is a great source of comfort: with it a calm passage is to be made across many a bad night.
— NIETZSCHE

The real reason for not committing suicide is because you always know how swell life gets again after the hell is over. — HEMINGWAY

The calm, / Cool face of the river / Asked me for a kiss.
— LANGSTON HUGHES

Suicide, in fact, is a choice and an affirmation—of being.
— SARTRE

Just as I select my ship when I am about to go on a voyage, or my house when I propose to take a residence, so shall I choose my death when I am about to depart from life. — SENECA

SUPERIORITY and INFERIORITY

Superiority and inferiority are individual, not racial or national. — PHILIP WYLIE

No one can make you feel inferior without your consent. — ELEANOR ROOSEVELT

There is nothing noble about being superior to some other man. The true nobility lies in being superior to your previous self. — HINDUSTANI PROVERB

SYMBOLS

Nothing in life requires a symbol since it is clearly what it is. — JOHN CAGE

Yet gladly let us trust the valid symbol for a moment. It is all we need. — RANIER MARIA RILKE

THEORY

Dear friend, theory is all grey, / And the golden tree of life is green. — GOETHE

No theory is good except on condition that one uses it to go beyond. — ANDRE GIDE

THOUGHT and THINKING

And life in his mind gave him pleasure, such pleasure that pleasure was not the word. — SAMUEL BECKETT

The greatest thoughts are the greatest events.
— NIETZSCHE

A man able to think isn't defeated—even when he is defeated. — MILAN KUNDERA

Our finite thinking is always relative and thus can in some way justify everything. — KARL JASPERS

One thought fills immensity. — WILLIAM BLAKE

Of its own beauty is the mind diseased. — LORD BYRON

I am not absentminded. It is the presence of mind that makes me unaware of everything else.
— G. K. CHESTERTON

I think him so because I think him so.
— SHAKESPEARE

A man is known by the company his mind keeps.
— THOMAS BAILEY ALDRICH

My thought is *me*; that is why I can't stop. I exist by what I think...and I can't stop thinking. — SARTRE

You know these things as thoughts, but your thoughts are not your experiences, they are the echo and after-effect of your experiences: as when your room trembles after a carriage goes past. I however am sitting in the carriage, and often I am the carriage itself.

— NIETZSCHE

Sometimes I think; and sometimes *I am*.

— PAUL VALERY

I paint things the way I think them, not the way I see them.   — PICASSO

The mind is its own place, and in itself / Can make a heaven of Hell, a hell of Heaven.   — JOHN MILTON

Man is God by his faculty for thought.   — LAMARTINE

No two unthought things are alike. — EDMOND JABES

The actuality of thought is life.   — ARISTOTLE

A profound thought is in a constant state of becoming.

— CAMUS

The thinker needs nobody to refute him: for that he suffices himself.   — NIETZSCHE

The universe is change; our life is what our thoughts make it.   — MARCUS AURELIUS

There are no evil thoughts except one: the refusal to think.   — AYN RAND

All that we are is the result of what we have thought.

— SARTRE

TIME

Think'st thou existence doth depend on time? / It doth;
and actions are our epochs.　　　— LORD BYRON

Time is a notion entirely human in its origin and, in
fact, it does not exist.　　　— JEAN COCTEAU

Time is born in the eyes, everybody knows that.

— JULIO CORTAZAR

My field is time.　　　— GOETHE

All my possessions for a moment of time.

— ELIZABETH I (last words)

There is no time without man.　　　— HEIDEGGER

And he who conceives time or eternity as old is he who
has no consciousness of his own time or of his own
attainable eternity, he who does not conceive his
immanence, he who does not take into account or
understand his destiny.　　　— JUAN RAMON JIMENEZ

Nature's security is due to the fact that time has no
significance for it.　　　— KIERKEGAARD

Time and I against any two.　　　— SPANISH PROVERB

Killing time and killing yourself amounts to the same
thing, strictly speaking.　　　— ELSA TRIOLET

I recommend you to take care of the moments: for the hours will take care of themselves.
— LORD CHESTERFIELD

Time is not a line, but a series of now points.
— TAISEN DESHIMARU

To realize the unimportance of time is the beginning of wisdom.
— BERTAND RUSSELL

As if you could kill time without injuring eternity.
— THOREAU

The mind of man works with strangeness upon the body of time. An hour, once it lodges in the queer element of the human spirit, may be stretched to fifty or a hundred times its clock length; on the other hand, an hour may be accurately represented by the timepiece of the mind by one second.
— VIRGINIA WOOLF

The butterfly counts not days but moments, / And has time enough.
— RABINDRANATH TAGORE

I don't ask for your pity, but just your understanding—no, not even that—no. Just for your recognition of me in you, and the enemy, time, in us all.
— TENNESSEE WILLIAMS

If time frightens us, it is because it works out the problem and the solution comes afterwards.
— CAMUS

TRAGEDY

Forget your personal tragedy. We are all bitched from the start and you especially have to be hurt like hell before you can write seriously. But when you get the damned hurt use it—don't cheat with it.

— HEMINGWAY

Life can be magnificent and overwhelming—that is its whole tragedy. Without beauty, love, or danger, it would be almost easy to live.
— CAMUS

There are two tragedies in life. One is not to get your heart's desire. The other is to get it. — BERNARD SHAW

Tragedy is clean, it is restful, it is flawless.
— JEAN ANOUILH

We begin to live when we have conceived life as tragedy.
— WILLIAM BUTLER YEATS

TRUTH

From the evening breeze to this hand on my shoulder, everything has its truth.
— CAMUS

I am the only real truth I know.
— JEAN RHYS

Life without truth is not possible. Truth is perhaps life itself.
— KAFKA

If truth is a value it is because it is true and not because it is brave to speak it.
— W. SOMERSET MAUGHAM

Truth disappears with the telling of it.
— LAWRENCE DURRELL

Truth has no special time of its own. Its hour is now—always.
— ALBERT SCHWIETZER

Whatever truth there is, is mine.
— SENECA

Truth is that which does not disturb the pattern of what we already know.
— NORTHROP FRYE

What remains strange and incomprehensible to us is a limit to our own truth.
— KARL JASPERS

Not everyone can see the truth, but he can *be* it...
— KAFKA

Truth is a matter of direct apprehension—you can't climb a ladder of mental concepts to it.
— LAWRENCE DURRELL

I am not seeking what is universal, but what is true.
— CAMUS

There are truths that are not for all men, nor for all times.
— VOLTAIRE

Away with eternal truth. The truth lives from day to day, and the marvelous Plato of yesterday is chiefly bosh today.
— D.H. LAWRENCE

The truth of a thing is the feel of it, not the think of it.
— STANLEY KUBRICK

Truth, for any man, is that which makes him a man.
— SAINT-EXUPERY

The truth, my friends, is not eloquent, except unspoken; its vast shadow lends eloquence to our sparks of thought as they die into it.   — SANTAYANA

A man is always prey to his truths.   — CAMUS

The great enemy of the truth is very often not the lie—deliberate, contrived and dishonest—but the myth—persistent, persuasive and unrealistic.
— JOHN F. KENNEDY

Such is the irresistible nature of truth that all it asks, and all it wants, is the liberty of appearing.
— THOMAS PAINE

True words always seem paradoxical but no other form of teaching can take their place.   — LAO TSE

UNDERSTANDING

Every profound thinker is more afraid of being understood than of being misunderstood.   — NIETZSCHE

When you try to understand everything, you will not understand anything. The best way is to understand yourself, and then you will understand everything.
— SHUNRYU SUZUKI

If you understand, things are just as they are. If you do not understand, things are just as they are.

— ZEN BUDDHIST SAYING

It's taken me all of my life to understand that is not necessary to understand everything. — RENE COTY

Only one man ever understood me. And he didn't understand me. — HEGEL (last words)

A man of understanding has lost nothing, if he has himself. — MONTAIGNE

UNHAPPINESS

I have the true feeling of myself only when I am unbearably unhappy. — KAFKA

I have discovered that all of man's unhappiness derives from only one source—not being able to sit quietly in a room. — PASCAL

If artists and poets are unhappy, it is after all because happiness does not interest them. — SANTAYANA

I've had an unhappy life, thank God.

— RUSSELL BAKER

The UNKOWABLE

Penetrating so many secrets, we cease to believe in the unknowable. But there it sits nevertheless, calmly licking its chops.　　　　　　　— H.L. MENCKEN

A sad wind came, from invisible worlds... / And she, she asked me about things unknowable / And I answered her with unattainable things.
　　　　　　　　　　— JUAN RAMON JIMENEZ

The UNKNOWN

My eyes are useless, for they render back only the image of the known.　　　　　　　— HENRY MILLER

Whoever starts out toward the unknown must consent to venture alone.　　　　　　　— ANDRE GIDE

I fear the known more than the unknown.
　　　　　　　　　　　　— PAUL VALERY

Nothing puzzles me more than time and space; and yet nothing troubles me less.　　　　— CHARLES LAMB

Let's give ourselves up to the unknown, not out of desperation but to plumb the deep pits of the absurd.
　　　　　　　　　　　　— F.T. MARINETTI

VIOLENCE

Beauty is unattainable to all violent wills.
　　　　　　　　　　　　— NIETZSCHE

In violence we forget who we are. — MARY McCARTHY

Violence is essentially wordless. — THOMAS MERTON

The study of crime begins with the knowledge of one-self. — HENRY MILLER

WILL

The will is a creator. — NIETZSCHE

To be is to will and so is to become. — D.T. SUZUKI

Man would rather will *nothingness* than not will.
— NIETZSCHE

To will is to stir up paradoxes. — CAMUS

Let my will take the place of reason. — JUVENAL

Determination is also a solitude. — CAMUS

Will cannot be quenched against its will. — DANTE

But reason is only reason, and it can only satisfy the reasoning ability of man, whereas volition is a manifestation of the whole of life. — DOSTOEVSKY

WISDOM

All wisdom comes out of one center, and the number of wisdom is one. — PARACELSUS

Growth in wisdom may be exactly measured by decrease in bitterness.　　　　　　　　— NIETZSCHE

Wisdom requires no form: her beauty must vary, as varies the beauty of the flame. She is no motionless goddess, for ever couched on her throne.

　　　　　　　— MAURICE MAETERLINCK

Not to know certain things is a great part of wisdom.

　　　　　　　　　　　— HUGO GROTIUS

You can't know wisdom, you have to *be* it.— RAM DASS

Not by years but by disposition is wisdom acquired.

　　　　　　　　　　　　— PLAUTUS

WORDS

Our words must seem to be inevitable.

　　　　　　— WILLIAM BUTLER YEATS

Every utterance is an event, and no two events are exactly alike. The extreme view, therefore, is that no word means the same thing twice.　　　— LOUIS SALOMAN

People to whom nothing has happened / Cannot understand the unimportance of words.　　　— T.S. ELIOT

Words are *possible* meanings, but they say nothing.

　　　　　　— JOSE ORTEGA Y GASSETT

No word is by nature.　　　　　　— ARISTOTLE

Basic words are spoken with one's being.

— MARTIN BUBER

Words are a form of action, capable of influencing change. Their articulation represents a complete, lived experience. — INGRID BENGIS

Yes, I have a native land: the French language.

— CAMUS

Yet no one hears his own remarks as prose.

— W.H. AUDEN

When an idea is wanting, a word can always be found to take its place. — GOETHE

At bottom one must lock oneself up before one's best words and go into solitude. The word must become flesh. That is the world's secret. — RANIER MARIA RILKE

The Universe will be our vocabulary.

— Motto of the Futurist Cinema, 1916

Summer afternoon—summer afternoon: to me those have always been the two most beautiful words in the English language. — HENRY JAMES

The poetry of words is quite as beautiful as that of sentences. — OLIVER WENDALL HOLMES

From one word to the other / what I say vanishes. / I know that I am alive / between two parentheses.

— OCTAVIO PAZ

In good writing, words become one with things.
— EMERSON

WRITERS and WRITING

The writer must write what he has to say, not speak it.
— HEMINGWAY

If you would be a writer, write.   — EPICTETUS

I write briefly. I can scarcely *be absent* for long.
— RENE CHAR

No poet or novelist wishes he were the only one who ever lived, but most of them wish they were the only one alive, and quite a number fondly believe their wish has been granted.   — W.H. AUDEN

A writer is a foreign country.   — MARGUERITE DURAS

I write to discover what I think.   — DANIEL BOORSTIN

Writing is a certain way of wanting freedom. — SARTRE

When you're writing, a kind of instinct comes into play. What you're going to write is already out there in the darkness.   — MARGUERITE DURAS

An original writer is not one who imitates nobody, but one whom nobody can imitate.
— VICOMTE de CHATEAUBRIAND

At the center of my work there lies an invincible sun.

— CAMUS

It is my ambition to say in ten sentences what everyone else says in a book—what everyone else does *not* say in a book. — NIETZSCHE

I write for myself and for strangers. The strangers, dear Readers, are an afterthought. — GERTRUDE STEIN

Perhaps writing means overcoming all resemblances within the very heart of resemblance, being finally like yourself, like nothing. — EDMOND JABES

Better to write for yourself and have no public, than to write for the public and have no self.

— CYRIL CONNOLLY

To write is to write is to write is to write is to write is to write is to write. — GERTRUDE STEIN

If I had to give young writers advice, I would say don't listen to writers talking about themselves.

— LILLIAN HELLMAN

I don't write fiction. I invent facts.

— JORGE LUIS BORGES

Writing, at its best, is a lonely life. — HEMINGWAY

"YES"

To say yes, you have to sweat and roll up your sleeves and plunge both hands into life up to the elbows. It is easy to say no, even if saying no means death.
                                                    — JEAN ANOUILH

The absurd man says yes and his effort will henceforth be unceasing.   — CAMUS

I have become one who blesses and one who says Yes.
                                                    — NIETZSCHE

i imagine that yes is the only living thing.
                                                    — e.e. cummings

Only one like myself who has opened his mouth and spoken, only one who has said yes, yes, yes, and again yes! can open wide his arms to death and know no fear!
                                                    — HENRY MILLER

...a sacred Yes is needed, my brothers, for the sport of creation.   — NIETZSCHE

I have said yes to everything. In that way suffering becomes an enchantment, and death—it is only an ingredient in the sweetness of life.   — KAFKA

But if you travel far enough, one day you will recognize yourself coming down the road to meet yourself. And you will say Yes.   — UNKNOWN

You can't say "Yes" without saying "I."   — AYN RAND

In acknowledging the No of eternity, I am saying Yes to life.   — THOMAS E. KELLY

Into all abysses do I carry my consecrating declaration Yes.   — NIETZSCHE

AUTHOR INDEX

Bacon, Francis (1561-1626). English philosopher and essayist. 3; 129.

Bailey, Philip James (1816-1902). English poet. 57.

Baker, Russell (1925-). American journalist. 94; 143.

Baldwin, James (1924-1987). American novelist and essayist. 63.

Balzac, Honoré de (1799-1850). French novelist. 107.

Barnes, Djuna (1892-1982). American novelist and playwright. 30.

Barrie, James Matthew (1860-1937). Scottish novelist. 110.

Barzun, Jacques (1907-). American critic. 106.

Baxter, Anne (1923-1985). American actress. 68.

Beauvoir, Simone de (1908-). French novelist. 15; 47; 84; 105; 112; 125.

Becker, May Lamberton (1873-1958). American editor, author, and critic. 4.

Beckett, Samuel (1906-1989). Irish-born French novelist and playwright. 7; 18; 24; 25; 40; 53; 69; 81; 91; 92; 93; 136.

Beethoven, Ludwig van (1770-1827). German composer. 40; 44.

Benchley, Robert (1889-1945). American humorist. 66; 131.

Bengis, Ingrid. 147.

Berdyaev, Nicolai (1874-1948). Russian philosopher. 48.

Berenson, Bernard (1865-1959). American art critic. 6.

Berger, John (1926-). British author and critic. 123.

Beryman, John (1914-1972). American poet and novelist. 45.

Betti, Ugo (1892-1953). Italian playwright. 39.

Bibesco, Elizabeth. 51.

Blake, William (1757-1827). English poet. 2; 37; 64; 97; 110; 136.

Blondel, Maurice (1861-1949). French philosopher. 8.

Boethius (c. 500). Roman philosopher. 87.

Bonaparte, Napoléon (Napoléon I) (1769-1821). Emperor of France. 21; 45.

Bonnard, Pierre (1867-1947). French painter. 101.

Bono, Edward de. 81.

Boorstin, Daniel (1914-   ). American writer. 148.

Borges, Jorge Luis (1899-1986). Argentine poet. 29; 76; 149.

Borman, Frank. 97.

Bowen, Elizabeth (1899-1973). Anglo-Irish novelist. 7.

Braque, Georges (1882-1963). French painter. 31.

Brecht, Bertolt (1898-1956). German playwright. 27; 39.

Bronte, Emily (1818-1848). English novelist and poet. 122.

Browning, Robert (1812-1889). English poet. 107.

Buber, Martin (1878-1965). Israeli philosopher. 67; 106; 109; 147.

Buchan, John (1875-1940). Scottish novelist and biographer. 9.

Buck, Pearl S. (1892-1973). American novelist. 112; 127; 131.

Buckrose, J. E. 75.

Buddha (Siddhartha Gautama) (c. 500 B.C.). Founder of the Buddhist philosophy. 63.

Buñuel, Luis (1900-1983). Spanish-Mexican surrealist film director. 9.

Buson (1716-1784). Japanese painter and haiku poet. 51.

Butler, Samuel (1835-1902). English novelist. 70.

Byrne, David (1952-   ). American lyricist and musician. 74.

Byron, George Gordon (Lord Byron) (1788-1824). English poet. 57; 117; 123; 136; 138.

Caesar, Caius Julius (100-44 B.C.). Roman emperor and general. 61.

Cage, John (1912-   ). American composer. 4; 22; 36; 38; 82; 90; 91; 93; 96; 101; 111; 124; 135.

Camus, Albert (1913-1960). French novelist and philosopher. 5; 7; 11; 13; 15; 21; 23; 24; 25; 35; 39; 40; 41; 42; 43; 44; 45; 47; 49; 52; 53; 55; 57; 60; 63; 64; 65; 68; 69; 71; 72; 73; 77; 78; 80; 82; 84; 91; 92; 99; 100; 101; 104; 106; 108; 109; 114; 115; 116; 121; 123; 125; 132; 133; 134; 137; 139; 140; 141; 142; 145; 147; 149; 150.

Carlyle, Thomas (1795-1881). English prose writer. 57; 58; 118; 124; 131.

Cather, Willa (1873-1947). American novelist. 83.

Céline, Louis-Férdinand (1894-1961). French novelist. 80.

Cervantes, Miguel de (1547-1616). Spanish novelist and poet. 118.

Cézanne, Paul (1839-1906). French painter. 18; 82; 88; 97.

Chamfort, Sébastien (1741-1794). French writer. 52.

Char, René (1907-1988). French poet. 3; 10; 23; 24; 37; 41; 44; 47; 65; 92; 95; 102; 108; 113; 148.

Chase, Alexander. 50.

Chateaubriand, Vicomte François René de (1768-1848). French writer. 148.

Chesterfield, Lord Philip (1694-1773). English diplomat and writer. 101; 139.

Chesterton, Gilbert Keith (1874-1936). English novelist and poet. 17; 44; 52; 136.

Chestov, Leo. 103.

Chuang Tzu (c. 300 B.C.). Chinese philosopher. 18.

Churchill, Winston (1874-1965). Prime Minister of Great Britain. 16; 128.

Cicero, Marcus Tullius (106-43 B.C.). Roman orator. 21; 23; 48.

Clarke, John. 35.

Cocteau, Jean (1889-1963). French poet, novelist, playwright, and cinematographer. 2; 46; 49; 64; 67; 81; 89; 97; 102; 128; 138.

Colette, Sidonie Gabrielle (1873-1954). French novelist. 54.

Colton, Charles Caleb (1780-1832). English writer. 127.

Congreve, William (1670-1729). English playwright. 36; 74.

Connolly, Cyril (1903-1974). English essayist and critic. 48; 149.

Conrad, Joseph (1857-1924). English novelist. 6; 22; 25.

Corneille, Pierre (1606-1684). French playwright. 117.

Cortázar, Julio (1914-1984). Argentine novelist, poet, and short-story writer. 53; 158.

Coty, René (1882-1962). French statesman. 143.

Cudlipp, Hugh (1913-   ). British journalist. 70.

Cummings, Edward Estlin (1894-1962). American poet. 59; 61; 150.

Curie, Marie (1867-1934). French scientist. 46.

Dahlberg, Edward (1900-1977). American novelist. 91.

Dante (Dante Aligheri) (1265-1321). Italian poet. 145.

Darwin, Charles (1809-1882). English naturalist and scientist. 86.

Dass, Ram (1931-   ). American writer. 146.

Deffand, Marie de Vichy-Chamrond (1697-1780). French intellectual. 91.

Delacroix, Eugène (1799-1863). French painter. 9.

Demetrius of Phalerum (c. 300 B.C.). Greek orator. 130.

Descartes, René (1596-1650). French philosopher. 117.

Deshimuru, Taisen. 139.

Diderot, Denis (1713-1784). French novelist and philosopher. 99.

Disraeli, Benjamin (1804-1881). English writer. 21; 130.

Doddridge, Philip (1707-1751). English writer. 71.

Donne, John (1572-1631). English poet. 111; 122.

Dostoevsky, Fyodor (1821-1881). Russian novelist and philosopher. 9; 10; 12; 20; 23; 57; 60; 68; 73; 76; 103; 109; 110; 112; 126; 133; 134; 145.

Dryden, John (1631-1700). English poet. 54.

Durant, William (1885-1981). American philosopher and historian. 90.

Duras, Marguerite (1914-). French novelist. 65; 91; 148.

Durrell, Lawrence (1912-1990). Anglo-Irish novelist, poet, and playwright. 78; 141.

Dürrenmatt, Friedrich (1921-1990). Swiss playwright and novelist. 95.

Einstein, Albert (1879-1955). Swiss-American physicist. 125.

Eliot, George. (Marion Evans) (1819-1880). English novelist. 51.

Eliot, Thomas Stearns (1888-1965). English poet. 32; 63; 82; 146.

Elizabeth I (1533-1603). Queen of England and patron of the arts. 138.

Ellis, Havelock (1859-1939). English psychiatrist and essayist. 34.

Eluard, Paul (1895-1952). French poet. 25.

Emerson, Ralph Waldo (1803-1882). American poet, essayist, and philosopher. 1; 10; 11; 12; 14; 15; 16; 24; 45; 51; 52; 55; 56; 57; 68; 71; 72; 78; 79; 86; 94; 100; 102; 105; 109; 115; 119; 130; 132; 147.

Epictetus (c. 100) Greek philosopher. 36; 47; 116; 148.

Epicurus (341-270 B.C.). Greek philosopher. 26; 28; 44; 49; 53; 80; 123.

Erasmus, Desiderius (1466-1536). Dutch philosopher. 31.

Ertz, Susan (1894-1985). American writer. 60.

Euripedes (480-405 B.C.). Greek tragic playwright. 71.

Faulkner, William (1897-1962). American novelist. 129.

Feather, William. 6.

Fellini, Fedrico (1920-). Italian filmmaker. 13.

Fichte, Johan Gottlieb (1762-1814). German philosopher. 85.

Finley, John (1863-1940). American editor. 16.
Fitzgerald, Francis Scott (1896-1940). American novelist. 25; 75; 104; 112; 114; 120.
Flaubert, Gustave (1821-1880). French novelist. 7; 93.
Fontenelle, Bernard (1657-1757). French man of letters. 16.
Forster, Edward Morgan (1879-1970). English novelist. 15; 27; 30.
Fowler, Gene (1890-1960). American editor and author. 119.
Fowles, John (1926-   ). American novelist. 5.
France, Anatole (1844-1924). French novelist. 11; 17; 69.
Francis, Brendan. 73; 105.
Freud, Anna (1895-1982). Austro-British psychoanalyst. 24.
Freud, Sigmund (1856-1939). Austrian psychologist and founder of psychoanalysis. 69.
Frisch, Max (1911-1991). Swiss novelist and playwright. 37.
Fromm, Erich (1900-1980). German-American psychoanalyst and philosopher. 16; 27; 47; 67; 71; 74; 78; 85; 118.
Frost, Robert (1874-1963). American poet. 55.
Frye, Northrop (1912-1991). Canadian critic. 141.
Fuller, R. Buckminster (1895-1983). American engineer, inventor, and philosopher. 112.

Gaulle, Charles de (1890-1970). President of the Fifth Republic of France. 3.
Gershwin, George (1898-1937). American composer. 105.
Gibbon, Edward (1737-1794). English historian. 129.
Gibran, Kahlil (1883-1931). Syrian-American writer, poet, and painter. 35.
Gide, André (1869-1951). French novelist and essayist. 6; 30; 31; 35; 41; 55; 63; 64; 79; 82; 96; 104; 122; 126; 130; 135; 144.
Gilman, Charlotte Perkins (1860-1935). American author. 37.
Gissing, George (1857-1903). English novelist. 82.

Goethe, Johann Wolfgang von (1749-1832). German poet and playwright. 5; 6; 17; 19; 20; 26; 31; 33; 38; 59; 67; 70; 73; 75; 78; 79; 83; 87; 105; 106; 116; 117; 120; 127; 131; 135; 138; 147.

Goldberg, Natalie. 32; 128.

Golding, William (1911-). English novelist. 68.

Goldscheider, Ludwig. 96.

Goncourt, Edmond de (1822-1896) and Jules de (1830-1870). French writers. 9.

Goodman, Roy. 55.

Gordon, Barbara (1935-). American writer and producer. 1.

Gorky, Maxim. (1868-1936). Russian writer. 74; 78.

Gracián, Baltasar (1601-1658). Spanish writer. 77; 121.

Graham, Martha (1894-1991). American dancer and choreographer. 9; 126.

Grayson, David (1870-1946). American journalist. 15.

Guillen, Jorge (1893-1984). Spanish poet. 74.

Guitton, Jean. 50.

Hammarskjöld, Dag (1905-1961). Swedish statesman. 4; 45; 48; 114.

Hartley, Leslie Poles (1895-1972). English writer. 97.

Havoc, June (1916-1973). American actress. 17.

Hawkes, John (1925-). American novelist and playwright. 27; 29; 33; 59; 89; 98; 100.

Hawthorne, Nathaniel (1804-1864). American novelist and short-story writer. 85.

Hayes, Helen (1900-1993). American actress. 75.

Hazlitt, William (1778-1830). English essayist and critic. 116.

Hedley, Leslie Woolf. 94.

Hegel, Georg Friedrich Wilheim (1770-1831). German philosopher. 47; 58; 89; 108; 143.

Heidegger, Martin (1889-1976). German philosopher. 5; 35; 38; 39; 41; 62; 79; 91; 92; 93; 99; 138.

Heine, Heinrich (1797-1856). German poet. 87; 125.

Heller, Joseph (1923-   ). American novelist. 60.

Heller, Walter (1915-1987). American economist. 106.

Hellman, Lillian (1905-1984). American playwright. 13; 17; 22; 149.

Hemingway, Ernest (1899-1961). American novelist and short-story writer. 14; 27; 30; 33; 77; 84; 90; 113; 114; 120; 128; 131; 134; 140; 147; 149.

Henri, Robert (1865-1929). American painter. 10.

Heraclitus (c. 500 B.C.). Greek philosopher. 18; 30; 44; 68; 89; 130.

Herbert, George (1593-1633). English poet. 4; 76.

Herrick, Robert (1591-1674). English poet. 83.

Hesse, Hermann (1872-1962). German novelist. 33; 104; 107.

Hineu. 44.

Hoffman, Abbie (1936-   ). American activist. 2.

Holmes, John H. 88.

Holmes, Oliver Wendall (1841-1935). American jurist. 16; 24; 32; 63; 147.

Horace (65-8 B.C.). Roman poet. 88; 123.

Huang Po. 123.

Hubbard, Elbert (1856-1915). American writer. 43; 95.

Hughes, Langston (1902-1967). American poet. 100; 115; 134.

Hugo Grotius. 146.

Humboldt, Wilheim von (1767-1835). German philologist. 25.

Hume, David (1711-1776). Scottish philosopher. 99.

Huxley, Aldous (1894-1963). English novelist and essayist. 42; 62.

Ibsen, Henrik (1828-1906). Norwegian playwright and poet. 79; 82; 132.

Ingenieros, Jose (1877-1925). Argentine psychiatrist. 96.
Ingersoll, Robert Green (1833-1899). American lawyer. 3.

Jabès, Edmond (1912-1991). French writer. 4; 13; 30; 86;
    93; 120; 125; 132; 137; 149.
James, Henry (1843-1916). American novelist and short-
    story writer. 147.
James, William (1842-1910). American philosopher,
    physiologist, and psychologist. 129.
Jaspers, Karl (1883-1969). German philosopher. 13; 22;
    38; 42; 60; 66; 78; 84; 85; 93; 98; 108; 109; 136; 141.
Jiménez, Juan Ramon (1881-1958). Spanish poet. 3; 10;
    13; 15; 18; 41; 58; 61; 72; 83; 105; 108; 128; 138; 144.
Joachim, Joseph. Concert violinist. 47.
Johnson, Samuel (1709-1784). English essayist and poet.
    21; 105.
Jonson, Ben (1573-1637). English playwright and poet. 94.
Joubert, Joseph (1754-1824). French essayist. 4.
Jung, Carl (1875-1961). Swiss psychiatrist. 25; 95.
Juvenal (Decimus Junius Juvenalis) (c. 100). Roman sati-
    rist. 145.

Kabir. 43.
Kafka, Franz (1883-1924). Austrian novelist and short-
    story writer. 8; 13; 31; 40; 47; 67; 72; 84; 109; 126; 131;
    140; 141; 143; 150.
Kahlo, Frida (1910-1954). Mexican painter. 107.
Kant, Immanuel (1724-1804). German philosopher. 69; 77.
Kaufman, Bel. American novelist. 20.
Kaufmann, Walter (1921-1980). American writer. 52.
Kazantzakis, Nikos (1883-1957). Greek novelist and poet. 100.
Keats, John (1795-1821). English poet. 11; 12.
Keller, Helen (1880-1968). American writer. 133.
Kelly, Thomas Earl (1971-   ). American writer. 113; 151.

Kennedy, John Fitzgerald (1917-1963). American president. 142.

Kierkegaard, Søren (1813-1855). Danish philosopher. 20; 22; 28; 34; 37; 38; 54; 62; 80; 85; 90; 95; 99; 103; 113; 114; 127; 130; 138.

Killinger, John (1933-   ). American writer. 104.

Klee, Paul (1879-1940). Swiss painter. 9.

Koestler, Arthur (1905-1983). Hungarian novelist. 108.

Kubrick, Stanley (1928-   ). American film director. 141.

Kundera, Milan (1929-   ). Czech-born French novelist. 136.

La Bruyère, Jean de (1645-1696). French writer. 129.

La Fontaine, Jean de (1621-1695). French poet and fabulist. 28; 66.

LaForgue, Jules (1860-1887). French poet. 102.

Lamartine, Alphonse de (1790-1869). French poet. 137.

Lamb, Charles (1775-1834). English essayist. 144.

Lao-tse (604-531 B.C.). Chinese philosopher and founder of Taoism. 142.

Law, William (1686-1761). English writer. 104.

Lawrence, David Herbert (1885-1930). English novelist and short-story writer. 19; 47; 69; 85; 141.

Lee, Harper (1926-   ). American novelist. 22.

Leeuw, Aart van der. 68.

Legal maxim. 5.

LeGuin, Ursula Kroeber (1929-   ). American writer. 32.

Leonardo da Vinci (1452-1519). Italian artist, inventor, and scientist. 30; 71; 92; 97; 128.

Lessing, Doris (1919-   ). English writer. 34.

Lewis, D.B. Wyndham (1894-1969). English essayist and biographer. 43.

Lewis, Joseph. American writer. 68.

Lichtenberg, Georg Christoph (1742-1799). German physicist and writer. 120.

Lindbergh, Anne Morrow (1906-   ). American writer. 129.

Linssen, Robert. 108.

Lonergan, Bernard (1904-1984). Canadian writer. 99.

Loos, Anita (1893-1981). American author and screen-writer. 44.

Lourde, Audre. 121.

Lowell, James Russell (1819-1891). American poet and critic. 2.

Machiavelli, Niccolò (1469-1527). Florentine philoso-pher. 122.

MacLeish, Archibald (1892-1982). American poet. 102.

Maeterlinck, Maurice (1862-1949). Belgian poet and play-wright. 44; 130; 146.

Maharaj, Nisargadatta. 54.

Mallarmé, Stéphane (1842-1898). French poet. 100; 103.

Malraux, André (1901-1976). French novelist. 7; 26; 29; 31; 37; 43.

Mann, Thomas (1875-1955). German novelist. 22; 29; 44; 58.

Marcel, Gabriel (1889-1973). French philosopher. 103.

Marcus Aurelius (121-180). Roman emperor and philoso-pher. 10; 18; 19; 28; 36; 49; 69; 71; 83; 85; 99; 114; 117; 119; 120; 137.

Marcus Pacuvius (c. 200 B.C.). Greek poet. 100.

Marinetti, Filippo Tommaso (1876-1944). Italian writer. 144.

Markham, Beryl (1902-1986). English aviator and author. 96.

Marlowe, Christopher (1564-1593). English dramatist and poet. 76.

Marx, Karl (1818-1883). German philosopher. 31.

Maugham, William Somerset (1874-1965). English nov-elist and playwright. 11; 126; 140.

Maurois, André (1885-1967). French novelist and biog-rapher. 92.

Maxwell, William (1908-   ). American writer. 54.

McCarthy, Mary (1912-1989). American novelist and critic. 145.

Melville, Herman (1819-1891). American novelist and short-story writer. 86.

Menander (342-292 B.C.). Greek playwright. 30.

Mencken, Henry Louis (1880-1956). American writer. 8; 144.

Merton, Thomas (1915-1968). French poet. 145.

Michelangelo (1475-1564). Italian sculptor, painter, architect, and poet. 35.

Millay, Edna St. Vincent (1892-1950). American poet. 20; 76; 83.

Miller, Arthur (1915-   ). American novelist and playwright. 104.

Miller, Henry (1891-1980). American novelist. 9; 14; 15; 18; 19; 23; 33; 50; 64; 70; 83; 84; 98; 115; 128; 144; 145; 150.

Milton, John (1608-1674). English poet. 82; 109; 137.

Mireilles, Edith. 42.

Molière (Jean Baptiste Poquelin) (1622-1673). French playwright. 66.

Montaigne, Michel de (1533-1592). French philosopher and essayist. 48; 80; 107; 116; 119; 143.

Montesquieu, Charles, Baron de (1689-1755). French philosopher. 54; 111.

Morley, Christopher (1890-1957). American novelist and essayist. 104; 133.

Munthe, Alex. 122.

Murdoch, Iris (1919-   ). British novelist and philosopher. 8.

Nabokov, Vladimir (1899-1977). Russian-American novelist. 7.

Navajo refrain. 12.

Neruda, Pablo (1904-1973). Chilean poet. 89; 102.

Nevelson, Louise (1900-1988). Russian-American sculptor. 25.

Newman, John Henry (1801-1890). English writer. 17.
Nicholson, Harold (1886-1968). English essayist and
    critic. 4.
Niebuhr, Reinhold (1892-1971). American theologian. 88; 113.
Nietzsche, Friedrich (1844-1900). German philosopher.
    3; 5; 6; 7; 8; 10; 11; 13; 16; 17; 18; 19; 24; 26; 28; 32; 33;
    36; 39; 43; 44; 46; 48; 49; 50; 51; 52; 54; 55; 57; 58; 60;
    62; 65; 66; 67; 70; 73; 75; 76; 77; 80; 81; 84; 85; 86; 88;
    89; 93; 98; 103; 110; 111; 112; 114; 117; 121; 123; 124;
    126; 129; 132; 133; 134; 136; 137; 142; 144; 145; 146;
    149; 150; 151.
Nin, Anaïs (1914-1977). French-American novelist. 49;
    68; 74; 109.

O'Hara, Frank (1926-1966). American poet. 59; 102.
O'Neill, Eugene (1888-1953). American playwright. 73; 128.
O'Keefe, Georgia (1887-1986). American painter. 118.
Ortega y Gasset, José (1883-1955). Spanish philosopher.
    1; 21; 50; 71; 75; 146.

Paine, Thomas (1737-1809). English revolutionist. 142.
Paracelsus, Philippus Aureolus (1493-1541). Swiss alche-
    mist and physician. 94; 145.
Pascal, Blaise (1623-1662). French philosopher. 3; 42; 85;
    88; 94; 95; 99; 118; 120; 130; 143.
Pavase, Cesare (1908-1950). Italian novelist and poet. 84.
Paz, Octavio (1914-   ). Mexican poet and essayist. 5; 21;
    26; 90; 97; 147.
Perk, Jacques. 12.
Perkins, Maxwell. (1884-1947). American editor. 14.
Persius (Aulus Persius Fluccus). (A.D. 34-62). Roman sa-
    tirical poet. 123.
Petronius, Gaius (c. A.D. 65). Roman satirical novelist
    and poet. 45.

Phillips, Wendall (1811-1884). American activist. 81.

Picasso, Pablo (1881-1949). Spanish painter and sculptor. 7; 59; 115; 137.

Pindar (518-438 B.C.). Greek poet. 59; 103.

Plath, Sylvia (1932-1963). American poet. 28.

Plato (428-347 B.C.). Greek philosopher and writer. 110.

Plautus (254-184 B.C.). Roman comic playwright. 45; 146.

Pliny the Elder (Caius Plinius Secundus) (A.D. 23-79). Latin writer and scientist.

Poe, Edgar Allen (1809-1849). American poet and short-story writer. 9; 61.

Ponge, Francis (1899-1988). French poet and essayist. 79; 87.

Porchia, Antonio (1886-?). Argentine writer. 31; 51; 76.

Powell, Anthony (1905-   ). English novelist. 121.

Prévert, Jacques (1900-1977). French poet and screenwriter. 110.

Protagorus. 79.

Proust, Marcel (1871-1922). French novelist. 33; 58; 76; 89; 101; 109; 112; 133.

Proverbs, Chinese. 12.

Proverbs, French. 81; 96.

Proverbs, German. 87.

Proverbs, Greek. 90.

Proverbs, Hindu. 135.

Proverbs, Irish. 72; 116.

Proverbs, Italian. 73, 104.

Proverbs, Latin. 82; 132.

Proverbs, Spanish. 19; 91; 138.

Publius Syrus (c. 100 B.C.). Latin writer. 61.

Racine, Jean Baptiste (1639-1699). French playwright. 75; 131.

Ramuz, Charles-Férdinand (1878-1947). Swiss novelist. 11.

Rand, Ayn (1905-1982). American novelist and philosopher. 2; 23; 25; 52; 56; 65; 72; 76; 77; 78; 80; 84; 86; 88; 119; 122; 125; 137; 150.

Reid, Alistair (1926-   ). American poet and writer. 20.

Reik, Theodor (1888-1969). American psychologist and writer. 74.

Renan, Ernest (1823-1892). French writer and critic. 131.

Renard, Jules (1864-1910). French novelist and playwright. 81.

Rénoir, Pierre Auguste (1841-1919). French painter. 107.

Repplier, Agnes (1855-1950). American essayist and biographer. 55.

Rhys, Jean (1894-1979). English novelist and short-story writer. 140.

Rich, Adrienne (1929-   ). American poet. 17.

Richter, Jean Paul (1763-1825). German novelist. 90.

Rilke, Ranier Maria (1875-1926). German poet. 27; 31; 32; 45; 50; 62; 64; 76; 77; 91; 108; 109; 135; 147.

Rimbaud, Jean Nicolas Arthur (1854-1891). French poet. 62.

Rivers, Larry (1923-   ). American painter. 7.

Robbe-Grillet, Alain (1922-   ). French novelist, essayist, and filmmaker. 87.

Rochefoucauld, François, Duc de la (1613-1680). 16; 96; 98; 106; 131.

Roethke, Theodore (1908-1963). American poet. 26; 34; 38; 94; 125; 132.

Roosevelt, Eleanor (1884-1962). American humanitarian. 135.

Roosevelt, Theodore (1858-1919). American president.

Rorem, Ned (1923-   ). American composer. 7.

Rousseau, Jean-Jacques (1712-1778). French philosopher. 31; 62; 117; 124.

Ruggiero, Guidore (1944-   ). American historian. 41.

Rumi (Jalal ud-din Rumi) (1207-1273). Persian poet. 32; 86.

Ruskin, John (1819-1900). English writer. 21; 63.

Russell, Bertrand (1872-1970). English philosopher. 29; 46; 53; 56; 79; 139.

Saint-Beuve, Charles Augustin. 120.

Saint-Exupéry, Antoine de (1900-1944). French novelist and aviator. 2; 20; 27; 40; 46; 65; 70; 71; 74; 77; 106; 113; 115; 127; 142.

Saloman, Louis. 146.

Samurai maxim. 3.

Sand, George (Amandine Lucile Aurore Dupin) (1804-1876). French writer. 55.

Sandburg, Carl (1878-1967). American poet. 102.

Santayana, George (1863-1952). Spanish-American writer and philosopher. 8; 10; 12; 15; 27; 34; 35; 53; 54; 56; 58; 61; 64; 65; 70; 98; 103; 111; 113; 142; 143.

Sarraute, Nathalie (1900-   ). French novelist. 121.

Sarton, May (1912-   ). American poet and novelist. 6; 94.

Sartre, Jean-Paul (1905-1980). French novelist, philosopher, and playwright. 2; 5; 9; 10; 19; 20; 23; 26; 28; 30; 33; 37; 38; 39; 40; 41; 42; 47; 48; 57; 59; 66; 67; 70; 71; 77; 78; 85; 87; 92; 97; 98; 103; 107; 109; 112; 113; 127; 129; 134; 136; 138; 148.

Schiller, Johann Christoph Friedrich von (1759-1805). German playwright and poet. 16; 38; 45; 55.

Schopenhauer, Arthur (1788-1860). German philosopher. 47; 59; 91; 128.

Schrodinger, Erwin (1887-1961). Austrian physicist and writer. 104.

Schwietzer, Albert (1875-1965). French philosopher. 141.

Scott-Maxwell, Florida. 36.

Seneca (4 B.C.- A.D. 65). Roman philosopher and playwright. 27; 28; 68; 79; 116; 122; 134; 141.

Service, Robert (1874-1958). Canadian writer. 54.

Servin, Michel. 66.

Shakespeare, William (1564-1616). English playwright. 2; 28; 37; 52; 69; 74; 85; 91; 94; 97; 121; 123; 126; 136.

Shaw, George Bernard (1856-1950). Irish playwright and critic. 34; 42; 56; 106; 107; 110; 112; 117; 140.

Sheldon, William Herbert (1898-1977). American psychologist. 55.

Shelley, Percy Bysshe (1792-1822). English poet. 116.

Skowacki, Juliusz. 51.

Smith, Elinor (1917-   ). American writer. 1.

Smith, Logan Pearsall (1865-1946). English writer. 49; 72.

Socrates (470-399 B.C.). Greek philosopher. 68.

Sontag, Susan (1933-   ). American essayist and novelist. 8.

Sophocles (496-406 B.C.). Greek tragic playwright. 79; 119; 130.

Spinoza, Benedict (1632-1677). Dutch philosopher. 56.

Sri Aurobindo. 65.

Sri Ramakrishna. 30.

Staël, Germaine de (1766-1817). French writer. 69.

Stafford, William (1914-1993). American poet. 87.

Stein, Gertrude (1874-1946). American poet and novelist. 4; 17; 29; 37; 46; 50; 60; 113; 119; 133; 149.

Steinem, Gloria (1934-   ). American journalist. 110.

Stendahl (Marie Henri Beyle) (1783-1842). French novelist and critic. 112.

Stevenson, Robert Louis (1850-1894). Scottish novelist and poet. 3; 4; 56; 70; 100.

Stirner, Max (1806-1856). German philosopher. 57.

Stoppard, Tom (1937-   ). English playwright and novelist. 29; 32.

Strand, Mark (1934-   ). American poet, essayist, and short-story writer. 30; 39; 82.

Stravinsky, Igor (1882-1971). Russian-American composer. 8; 105.

Styron, William (1925-   ). American novelist. 39.

Suzuki, Daisetz Teitaro (1870-1966). Japanese philosopher and writer. 145.

Suzuki, Shunyru. 142.

Swift, Jonathan (1667-1745). English satirist. 72.

Szasz, Thomas (1920-   ). American psychiatrist and author. 118; 123.

Szent-Györgyi, Albert (1893-1986). Hungarian-American biochemist and writer. 34.

Tagore, Rabindranath (1861-1941). Bengali poet, novelist, and composer. 139.

Tao Te Ching. 95.

Tauler, Johannes. 92.

Tennyson, Alfred (1809-1892). English poet. 16; 43; 59; 75.

Terence (Publius Terentius Afer) (195-159 B.C.). Roman playwright. 49; 110.

Theobald, Lewis (1688-1744). English essayist and playwright. 59.

Thomas, Dylan (1914-1953). Welsh poet. 77; 102; 125.

Thompson, Dorothy (1894-1961). American journalist and author. 35.

Thoreau, Henry David (1817-1862). American essayist and poet. 37; 55; 66; 79; 95; 107; 122; 125; 127; 132; 133; 139.

Tillich, Paul (1886-1965). American philosopher. 73; 96.

Tocqueville, Alexis de (1805-1859). French political leader and writer. 95.

Tolstoy, Leo (1828-1910). Russian novelist and philosopher. 54; 119.

Triolet, Elsa (1896-1970). French novelist. 138.

Turgenev, Ivan Sergeyevich (1818-1883). Russian novelist. 111.

Twain, Mark (Samuel Clemens) (1835-1910). American writer. 26; 46; 86; 88; 111.

Tynan, Kenneth (1927-   ). English drama critic. 71.

Tzara, Tristan (Andrei Codrescu) (1946-   ). American novelist and poet. 13.

Unamuno, Miguel de (1864-1936). Spanish philosopher, poet, and novelist. 38; 51; 53; 61; 93.

Valéry, Paul (1871-1945). French poet. 11; 23; 29; 51; 62; 64; 87; 89; 92; 97; 103; 110; 118; 124; 127; 137; 144.

Van der Post, Laurens. 101.

Van Gogh, Vincent (1853-1890). Dutch painter. 15.

Vansittart, Peter. 67.

Vauvenargues, Marquis de Luc de Clapiers (1715-1747). French philosopher. 1; 66.

Vian, Boris (1920-1959). French novelist. 56.

Vigny, Alfred de (1797-1863). French poet, playwright, and novelist. 129.

Virgil (Publius Vergilius Maro) (70-19 B.C.). Roman poet. 116.

Vogelweide, Walther von der. 75.

Voltaire (François Marie Arouet) (1694-1778). French satirist, essayist, and philosopher. 14; 30; 47; 88; 99; 101; 124; 127; 141.

Watts, Alan (1915-1973). American philosopher and writer. 88; 105.

Weiss, Peter. (1916-   ). German painter, novelist, and film director. 29.

Wells, Herbert George (1866-1946). English novelist. 24.

About the author

Thomas E. Kelly was born in Seattle, Washington, where he attended the University of Washington. He is currently working on his first contemporary novel.

ORDER FORM

Qty.	Title	Price	Can.Price	Total
	Wisdom of One	$12.95	$16.95	
			Subtotal	
	Shipping and Handling (add $3.00 for one book, $2.00 for each additional book)			
	Sales tax (WA residents only, add 8.2%)			
	Total Enclosed			

Telephone Orders:
Call 1-800-468-1994.
Have your VISA or
Mastercard ready.

FAX Orders:
1-206-672-8597. Fill out
order blank and fax.

Postal Orders:
Hara Publishing
P.O. Box 19732
Seattle, WA 98109

Payment: Please Check One:

☐ Check

☐ VISA

☐ MasterCard

Expiration Date: _____ / _____
Card #: _____
Name on Card: _____

NAME _____

ADDRESS _____

CITY _____ STATE _____ ZIP _____

DAYTIME PHONE _____

Quantity discounts are available, 206-672-8597.
Thank you for your order!

I understand that I may return any books for a full refund if not satisfied.